TALES OF THE OLD SOLDIERS

TALES OF THE OLD SOLDIERS

Ten Veterans of the First World War
Remember Life and Death in the Trenches

TOM QUINN

ALAN SUTTON

First published in the United Kingdom in 1993 by
Alan Sutton Publishing Limited
Phoenix Mill · Far Thrupp · Stroud · Gloucestershire

First published in the United States of America in 1993 by
Alan Sutton Publishing Inc.
83 Washington Street · Dover · NH 03820

British Library Cataloguing in Publication Data

Tales of the Old Soldiers
    I. Quinn, Tom
    940.4
    ISBN 0–7509–0090–3

Library of Congress Cataloging in Publication Data applied for

*Jacket illustrations: above: C Squadron of the Surrey Yeomanry at Poeuilly
Crossroad, March 1917 (photograph courtesy of the Imperial War
Museum); below: Oliver Andrews with a French farmer and his son who
was fighting with the French army.*

Typeset in 11/13 Bembo.
Typesetting and origination by
Alan Sutton Publishing Limited.
Printed in Great Britain by
The Bath Press, Avon.

The centuries will burn rich loads
With which we groaned,
Whose warmth shall lull their dreaming lids
While songs are crooned.
But they will not dream of us poor lads,
Lost in the ground.
WILFRED OWEN (1893–1918)

CONTENTS

ACKNOWLEDGEMENTS

It is impossible adequately to express my gratitude to the veterans who gave up so much of their time to talk to me about a subject that, in some cases, they find distressing to this day. All were unfailingly patient and polite even when I must have appeared remarkably obtuse!

I also owe a debt of gratitude to a number of individuals and institutions including L.P., S.J.G., B.O.F., Toby Buchan and the staffs of the Imperial War Museum and The British Library.

INTRODUCTION

It is more than three-quarters of a century since the Great War ended. In that time millions of words have been written about the futility and waste of that conflict, about the heroism of the young men who fought on both sides and about the far-reaching effects of a war so terrible that it was fondly imagined it would put an end to all future wars. It was as if we had been infected with some kind of national and international madness to allow such things to happen and it was impossible to believe that we could ever descend so low again. The sad idealism of that judgement bears witness to the depth of feeling at the time, the depth of feeling about the lost young men whose countless names survive on stone monuments in virtually every village and town in Britain.

But while we remember those who died, perhaps we should also remember the tens of thousands who returned from the front. Some were relatively unscathed, others badly wounded and permanently disabled. It was the experiences of these men, the stories they had to tell and the perception of them as national heroes that made post-1918 Britain so different from the cosy, idealistic, perhaps rather naïve world of Edwardian Britain. The war made many who had once accepted the old social order without question profoundly disillusioned and as a result society was changed utterly.

Of the thousands of men who returned in 1918 to pick up the threads of their lives, only a tiny number are still living today. No one knows exactly how many remain, but the number is rapidly decreasing and it will not be long before the Great War moves out into the darkness beyond living memory. All those who endured that war and survive to this day are in their nineties and by the end of this century they will be gone.

There are many firsthand published accounts of life in the trenches and the Imperial War Museum has done much to record the memories of those who are still alive, but when I began working on this book I felt that it was somehow in keeping with the nature of the war that a collection of interviews with veterans from different parts of the country should be published. I thought that I would be bringing these men together much as chance and the circumstances of war had thrown them together all those years ago.

This is not a study of one aspect of the war that uses men whose experiences illustrate that aspect; nor is it a thematic study; nor is it a book about men from one area, or about men who served in a particular regiment. I have simply brought together a handful of men whose only connection, other than their great age, is that they fought for the same cause long ago. Each has a different tale to tell; each has his own unique response to a singularly terrible conflict. Each man survived and had to come to terms with a return to a life that was never going to be the same again.

I have not attempted to clear up inconsistencies in their stories because time adds a patina to memory and the patina has a value since it is part of the way they now feel about their experiences. Their understanding of events has its own validity.

I think this is important partly because the growth of interest in the Great War among those who were born long after that conflict had ended, has, in a curious way, tended to increase what one is almost forced to describe as the romance of the thing; the Great War has taken on the aspect of a pure and almost holy sacrifice, which no doubt in some ways it really was. But away from the poppy fields and the almost unbearably poignant annual ceremony at the Cenotaph, the Great War lives not as sepia-coloured memory but, through its survivors, as flesh and blood – an appalling witness to the folly of man. The sense of folly and waste, the sense of human loss, is combined with the simple, quiet humanity of those who fought and survived.

The men who fought in the front line trenches, the junior officers and the soldiers, were told virtually nothing of what was happening until, in many cases, they discovered that they were being asked to do something that was unutterably stupid and that they were being asked to do it by men who had usually never been in a front line trench and had no idea, except in some theoretical way, what the war on the ground was like.

Take the example recounted by Bernard Martin, a subaltern on the Western Front, who describes the scene just before he led his men over the top. His commanding officer insisted, only one or two days before the battle was to start, that a number of men should go over the top without arms but blowing the charge on bugles. It was this same commanding officer who told Martin that his men were to go over the top and walk toward the enemy trenches in an orderly line at Passchendaele. It was as if the generals did not know – as Martin certainly did – that if even one German machine-gun were to survive the artillery barrage (which was highly likely), then most of his men would be mown down in the first few yards of their advance.

Martin also remembered a rare occasion when a general actually appeared in a front line trench. It was the first and only time in two years that this had happened in his experience. The general insisted that the men be given box periscopes instead of the far more useful – because shell-blast proof – folding mirrors already in use. It was as though the men in charge had a theory they were going to stick to whatever the situation in the actual fighting area. Martin was not impressed.

Field Marshal, Earl Haig, in overall charge of British forces, claimed that his every move was taken with divine help. He also believed that it was important not that an officer should *lead* his men to their deaths, but that he should *order* them to their deaths, a distinction that makes one gasp today. But rather than explicit statements of this kind, it was disenchantment with the ruling class, whose worth had been measured on the great battlefields of France and Belgium, that led to the popular belief that in the Great War the soldiers had been lions led by donkeys. It is certainly true that the generals never seemed to know exactly what was going on at the front and were never in any real danger themselves; they were simply convinced that their master plan – to destroy the enemy by heavy shelling – had to work because they believed it would.

The 'lions led by donkeys' idea developed out of disillusion. The idea that the sons of gentlemen were the natural leaders of the lower orders was challenged when the old order failed so badly on the battlefields of France and Flanders; it was time to kick over the traces and begin again with a new set of beliefs.

Among the veterans whose stories are told here, a majority believe that the war was conducted badly by old men who clung to ideas and tactics long out of date. Only two of the men take the opposite view that those in charge, Haig in particular, were not to blame and were, in fact, scapegoats for the terrible costs of a conflict that was otherwise inexplicable. If every village in the country had lost a cherished youngster, it had to be someone's fault and since those who ran the country also ran the war they must be to blame.

When we think of the idea of waste and folly in the Great War it is worth remembering the effect that an attack from the trenches could have. One survivor of the Somme described seeing

a wide upland slope, uniformly drab, dirty white, chalk mixed with decaying vegetation, not a tree stump or bush left, just desolation, with a track named Crucifix Alley for men to walk round or through shell holes to the large desolation of Delville Wood. The whole blasted slope dotted to the very edges with dead bodies, too many to bury, and too costly, the area being under constant fire from artillery. This awful display of dead men looked like a set piece, as though some celestial undertaker had spaced the corpses evenly for interment and then been interrupted. Several times I picked a way through this landscape of the unburied.

Men had to accept almost certain death or serious injury by walking out into no man's land against well-positioned overlapping machine-guns or, should terror get the better of them, they could refuse to go forward and be shot by an officer or face summary trial and execution by their own units. That said, most of those involved in what one might term 'virtual suicide' battles maintained that their training and sense of fellowship in the face of death with their comrades made it relatively rare for a man to show cowardice, regardless of the certainty of serious, often agonizing injury or even death in battle.

Another point to remember about infantrymen is that they did not normally get a chance to kill the enemy – they were simply asked to reach an objective and on the way they were subjected to enemy machine-gun and artillery fire. Men had to learn to watch their friends die, and for many that was the great fear – not the fact of dying, but the torment of witnessing that process so often in others.

And every day in the front line trenches there were casualties. A man might leave his comrades in one part of the trench, return moments later and find them all dead from a direct hit by a trench mortar or shell. The best a man could hope for in the infantry at Ypres or on the Somme was that he would walk until he was hit hard enough to bring him down without killing him and that he would then be picked up before he bled to death. The desire for a 'blighty' – a wound bad enough to get a man sent home – was both real and almost universal.

The chances of reaching one's objective when the troops went over the top were often minimal. An official German history (M. Gerster's *Die Schwaben an der Ancre*) describes the scene from the German side of the line:

It was vital to lose not a second in taking up position in the open to meet the British infantry who would advance immediately behind the artillery barrage. Looking towards the British trenches through the long trench periscopes there could be seen a mass of steel helmets above the parapet showing that the storm troops were ready for the assault. At 7.30 a.m. the hurricane of shells ceased as suddenly as it had started. Our men at once clambered up the steep shafts leading from the dug-outs to daylight and ran singly or in groups to the nearest shell craters. The machine-guns were pulled out of the dug-outs and hurriedly placed in position. A rough firing line was thus rapidly established. As soon as the men were in position a series of extended lines of infantry were seen moving forward from the British trenches. The first line appeared to continue without end right to left. It was quickly followed by a second and then a third and fourth. They came on at a steady, easy pace as if expecting to find nothing alive in our front trenches. The front line was now half way across no man's land. 'Get ready' was passed along our front from crater to crater and heads appeared over the crater edges as final positions were taken up for the best view. A few minutes later when the British front line was within 100 yards the rattle of machine-gun and rifle fire broke out along the whole line. Red rockets sped up into the sky as a signal to the artillery and a mass of shells from the German batteries in the rear tore through the air and burst among the advancing lines. Whole sections seemed to fall and the rear formations moving in close order quickly scattered. The advance rapidly crumbled under this hail of bullets and shells. All along the line men could be seen throwing up their arms and collapsing, never to move again. Badly wounded rolled about in their agony and others, less severely injured, crawled to the nearest shell hole for shelter. The extended lines, though badly shaken, now came on all the faster. Instead of a leisurely walk they covered the ground at the double. Within a few minutes the leading troops had advanced to within a stone's throw of our front trench and some of us continued to fire at point-blank range. Others threw hand grenades among them. The British bombers answered back while the infantry rushed forward with fixed bayonets. The noise of battle became indescribable. The shrill cheers as the British charged forward could be heard above the violent noise of machine-guns and bursting shells. With all this were mingled the moans and groans of the dying, the cries for help and the last screams of death. Again and again the extended lines of British infantry broke against the German defence like waves against a cliff only to be beaten back.

This account refers to the British assault on the main ridge up Ovillers Spur near Thiepval. Bernard Martin, who died in 1986, was at Albert on the Somme at about the same time. He made the following notes in his diary:

Ordered to attack enemy at Guillemont, came under heavy machine-gun fire before we got anywhere near objective. Dodged from shell hole to shell hole, but couldn't even see enemy gun emplacements. Had to abandon attack. Considerable casualties. In the afternoon battalion ordered to renew attack. Only field guns support available for us, too light to silence enemy machine-guns. Took cover when possible in shell holes, casualties heavy. Stretcher-bearers unable to evacuate wounded. Some died in silence, others screaming in agony. After advance of only a few yards had to lie low until dusk, then creep back. I lost a sergeant, two corporals and eight men killed as well as wounded.

This was the reality of fighting on the front, but it was conducted and ordered by men who were out of touch. At the time this was not seen as a bad thing – it was what generals were expected to do and it may therefore be harsh to judge the standards of one time by the standards of another. The wars of today are 'high tech' affairs in which individual men have to be accounted for at the highest level. In 1918 the life of the ordinary soldier was undoubtedly held cheaper than it is today. Patriotism in 1914–18 meant being prepared not to fight to order, but to die to order.

When men were injured during an advance some died quietly, some died screaming very loudly and in a way that could be quite terrifying for those still living. Often bodies had to be left unburied for days, particularly if they were enemy soldiers.

The common judgement even at quiet times in the trenches was that to be seen was to be shot. Newcomers carried away with the excitement of arriving at the front occasionally simply couldn't resist a peek over the top. The result, as often as not, was a bullet through the head and instant death.

It has been said that too much has been written of the horror of the trenches. I would disagree and say that if anything too much has been written about the way battles like the Somme developed as military manœuvres, and not as manœuvres involving individual human beings cut or blown to pieces. Too little has been written about how those battles were experienced by the ordinary soldiers who took part in them. Even the official account of the first Battle of the Somme, though couched in unemotional language, suggests the horror of the thing:

The position was in fact that of storming a fortress, in which according to precedent, there should be a main assault on the weakest spot, several other subsidiary ones on other possible weak spots, strong enough to be converted into main assaults and carried through, and also false assaults. Instead, the distribution of force was as uniform as the methods of attack were stereotyped. Men advanced at a walking pace and were mown down by the machine-gunners, strewing their bodies in no man's land. Battalions attacked in waves 100 yards apart in symmetrical lines, upright at a walking pace, rifles and bayonets held aslant in front of them. Men were cut down like corn as they advanced wave after wave.

They were easy targets. German snipers picked off the officers by their dress, Sam Browne belts and collar and tie, in the first few yards, while overhead the larks were singing. The first Battle of the Somme officially ended on 13 November 1916 in snow and blizzards on the Ancre. Total casualties in 1916 were given at British GHQ as 607,784. Official allied figures for the Somme were British 419,654, French 204,253. On the first day, 1 July, 19,000 British servicemen were killed outright and 57,000 were injured. It remains the greatest loss in a single day ever suffered by a British army, and the greatest suffered by any army in the First World War.

The British dead and wounded in the first Battle of the Somme swallowed up the heart of a generation. Nowhere was the advance more than 8 miles. The objectives laid down in Field Marshal Haig's orders for the first day were still unattained when winter closed in. The only gain was a narrow strip of blood-soaked ground which the Germans easily took back again in March 1918. A glorious victory had been expected, a terrible blood-bath had occurred. A most unsuitable place had been chosen for the attack; throughout the battle the British had the enemy above them in deep shelters, with machine-gun emplacements and excellent observation posts. Although Haig and his chief of staff drew up the plans for this great offensive, they never made any contact with the fighting men apart from motoring about behind the front from one corps HQ to another. The fact that the generals did not understand the war in which they were engaged is perhaps further evinced by their insistence that once the breakthrough came the cavalry would be used! To this end hundreds of thousands of horses were kept in France throughout the war waiting for the opportunity which never came. Even the official history (*Military Operations: France and Belgium, 1916*) comments dryly that 'The failures of the past were put down to reasons other than the stout use of the machine-gun by the enemy and his scientifically planned defences.'

What was true of the Somme was true of so many other battles in the Great War. Of course some men were lucky and fought in sectors – even on the Somme – where they reached their initial objectives quickly and with few casualties, but this was the exception rather than the rule. At Passchendaele, at Ypres and elsewhere the story is one of the sacrifice of tens of thousands of individual lives in battles that were directed by men who had learned their trade – if trade it can be called – on battlefields that were irrelevant to this war. It may be unfair to say that Haig was prepared to sacrifice any number of men because he believed that force of will would carry the day, but for many men the evidence of their own experience in the trenches weighs against any sympathy for Haig and we will be doing the survivors' accounts no justice if we refuse to accept the greater reality of individual experience on the front.

We have passed the stage when the ordinary man can somehow be sacrificed with impunity by a general who knows best even if he has no experience of the kind of warfare he is directing. Field Marshal Haig had his say in his own memoirs. Most of the soldiers who died had no chance to comment on the conflict that ended their lives, but their comrades who remain can now be heard.

If some of us are disgusted now that the generals should have been blamed for the Somme and Passchendaele how much greater must be our disgust to discover that General Smuts, reporting to the British cabinet about the failure of British forces at Passchendaele said that 'No one down to and including the corps commanders, was to blame. The fault lay entirely with the junior officers, the NCOs and the men.'

CHAPTER ONE

CLARRIE JARMAN

Clarrie Jarman is a rare survivor. Now ninety-seven, he was among the badly injured who lived – just – to tell the tale after that fateful morning in July 1916 when the first great Battle of the Somme began. Clarrie was born in Stoke Newington, north London, in 1896, but at the age of six months his parents took him and his two brothers away from the dense crowds of the big city, southwards to Woking, then a quiet country town in north Surrey. A slim, tall man of immense charm and great dignity, Clarrie still lives in Woking, and it was in Woking, in 1910, that he began his apprenticeship at a firm of ironmongers called Skeet and Jeffs.

I was bound to them for four years and I actually did three years and nine months. I only left because all the lads were joining up and I couldn't bear to be left out of it. It was the atmosphere of the times. You really did feel an intense enthusiasm to take part in what was seen as a glorious war.

My governor at the ironmongers wasn't too happy about me going, but as soon as I could I was off to see the recruiting officer. I told him I was eighteen, but he said you have to be nineteen to join up. He then asked how old I was again and, taking the hint, I said nineteen and I was in. It was only later, when the number of available men had dropped so drastically because of the enormous losses on the Western Front, that you were accepted at eighteen. Mind you, some lads managed to get in at sixteen because you didn't need to show a birth certificate or anything. If you told the recruiting officer you were nineteen, he believed you.

Having joined up I was made to form up with the other new recruits in the drill hall at Stoughton Barracks. I was put in the Queen's Royal West Surreys, which has now been amalgamated with the Hampshires. I was just a private in the infantry, the poor bloody infantry as they became known. I enjoyed the training, the comradeship – in fact, I enjoyed pretty much everything about army life.

At first, because so few uniforms and weapons were available, we were given long Lee Enfields. These were left-overs from the Boer War and not nearly as efficient as the short Lee Enfields we were eventually given. In fact, I was very sorry to part with my rifle when the time came.

I was one of the first hundred thousand who joined Kitchener's Army in August 1914. From Woking in Surrey, along with many other local lads, I was taken to Stoughton Barracks at Guildford, then a small, very rural place and also the depot for the Queen's Royal West Surrey Regiment. After just one night here I discovered that the 7th (Service) Battalion, The Queen's, had been formed. I was part of this and we were straight away transported to Purfleet in Essex.

There were no barracks or huts for us to go to, so from then until the end of December 1914 we were under canvas. The weather turned nasty and the camp, being near the River Thames, was soon flooded. We had to move out. Next we were taken off to Belus Park, at Averley in Essex. This was 4 miles from Purfleet. We were all disappointed to discover that here, too, we were to live under canvas. The battalion stayed here until January 1915 when we returned to Purfleet where huts had at last been built for us.

In April 1915 we were on the move yet again. This time to barracks in Colchester where, no sooner had we arrived, than we were off again on brigade manœuvres. We marched 18 long miles from Colchester to Ipswich where we stayed for one night in billets. Our manœuvres then took us across to Hollesley Bay on the wind-swept Suffolk coast. As I recall we were always having mock battles where the idea was to capture the men on the other side and prove that you'd done it by taking their rifle bolts. I remember we covered some 150 miles on foot on that occasion — much of it during the night — before returning to Ipswich after a week of living rough. Of course when you are young, as we were, this sort of thing is an adventure so we didn't mind. And it was all part of our training, but over the months to come we certainly put in some miles. We were in our billets in Ipswich by about 10 o'clock that night and then just one hour later the fall-in sounded and we had to march on through the night to Colchester. I remember how glad we were to get to our huts at Reedhall Camp, which we took over from the 10th Royal Fusiliers.

Towards the end of April 1915 we moved to Codford St Mary on Salisbury Plain for divisional manœuvres and rifle firing on the ranges. Occasionally an exercise would end in complete farce — I remember on Salisbury Plain during a torrential downpour we were trying to get our mules to pull the gun limbers and they just wouldn't do it. Eventually we had to give up and pull the bloody things ourselves! And those mules were expert kickers — they seemed to be able to kick backwards and forwards, but they usually worked hard and the men often became very fond of them.

This ended our training in England. It had taken a total of 11 months, much longer than was given to many other poor devils who joined up or were conscripted later on. At least we could say that we were well prepared.

About the end of June 1915 the 18th Division, which included my battalion, was ordered to France. As part of the 55th Brigade we embarked at Folkestone for Boulogne. Boulogne seemed rather quiet, I remember, but there were soldiers everywhere and we marched through the town to St Martin's Camp where we stayed for just one night. The thing that amazed me about that first march in France was the fact that all along the road young Frenchmen shouted at us, 'You gig-a-gig my sister for tin of bully!' I think they were rather hungry, poor devils. And there were prostitutes everywhere. It was a job to keep them out of our tents. After that one night we travelled to a place just outside Amiens by train and, from there, we marched to a village called Dernancourt, just behind the British front line. We then went into the front line for our first experience under fire, marching up through the village of Meaulte at night.

We took over a section of the line from the 1st Norfolks. The town of Albert was behind us and Fricourt, held by the Germans, in front. From that moment on we seemed to be under fire the whole time. At first when we heard the bullets whizzing by and the shells whining and bursting overhead we were ducking the whole time, but you soon get used to it and we learned how to tell the difference between bullets and shells that really were coming close and those that were almost certainly too far away to do us any harm. In fact it was a sort of badge of honour with us to treat the shells and bullets with contempt. With experience we learned when to take cover – and quickly – and when not. In the first days we sometimes didn't know whether we were ducking because our own shells were heading out over our heads towards the enemy or because we were the ones under attack.

During the rest of 1915 and all through the winter of 1915/16 we remained on this front between La Boisselle and a place called Suzanne, at the right of the British line and linking up with the French. That first winter was terrible, with snow and, at Christmas, rain, then bitter cold. At times the trenches became thick with mud and we were up to our knees in water for days on end which made life miserable, to say the least.

During this time the routine was to spend two weeks in the trenches and two weeks out and, with the mud and cold and ice, at least we knew that there would be little action − conditions made that impossible. I suppose our only real activity in those winter months was to send regular patrols and wiring parties at night into no man's land. Casualties were relatively few, but of course some lads were unlucky − they were shot at while out laying wires, or killed or badly wounded when shells or mortars landed in our trenches.

Our main food in the line was bully beef stew − bully beef was rather like corned beef − and we had to share one loaf a day between four men. Other than this we had a ration of cheese each day and some butter in tins. At night a dixie − a kind of big, open kettle − of tea and rum was sent up. For warmth we relied on charcoal braziers, one for each group of men in dug-outs. Charcoal was always burned as it gave off no smoke and therefore didn't give away our position. There were also tins of hard biscuits everywhere along the front − a bit like dog biscuits − and we could eat these whenever we liked. All day and all night in a front line trench you do two hours on and two off. A lot of the work was re-building after shell damage, although until the Somme I think we were on a fairly quiet part of the front. But having said that there was always a steady stream of casualties from snipers, mortars and occasional shells. I had one or two near misses early on, but nothing too bad. On one occasion during my first winter in the front line I was on duty with two friends and thought I'd better go and get my goatskin coat − we were issued with these because the weather was so bad. Anyway I went off, came back in two minutes and found my two friends dead. A direct hit from a shell.

When we were out of the line our time was always pretty fully occupied. First we had to clean the mud off uniforms and boots and clean buttons, rifles and equipment. We had to parade for a bath and change of underwear. The bath house was usually in some old barn and we had baths in tubs. We were hardly ever free of lice and, after being in the front line, our clothing was always riddled with them. There were rats everywhere too. They invaded the trenches; they came in droves to the villages; as we slept on lice-infested straw in old barns they ran over us all night.

Up on the firestep – the raised platform on the front of the trench – we used to have a bit of fun now and then by putting a piece of cheese on the end of our bayonets. A rat would soon come sniffing up and the one that got the cheese also got the bullet.

It wasn't all lying around waiting for something to happen – often a lad would be killed by a shell or machine-gun while out on a wiring party and if that happened his body was brought back and a man would have to stand guard over it all the rest of the night to keep the rats off. And he would have to be armed with a cudgel to do it. Next morning the poor devil would be buried. But there were amusing incidents too. I'll give you an example. I was with a friend in a front line trench with orders to detonate a series of mines we'd placed out in front of us in no man's land. We were supposed to detonate them if and when we saw the enemy coming. Anyway, there we were when along came a colonel. I had no idea he was a colonel and when he said to us, 'Are you sentries?' I replied, 'Well, we're not sandbags.' I discovered later from one of the junior officers that he'd gone along the trench saying to himself, 'I asked for that.' When I found out who he was I thought I'd be court martialled, but nothing ever happened.

When we were out of the line we had numerous other duties. We were on parade a lot of the time or sent on route marches or given physical jerks, as we used to call exercise sessions. But we also had various entertainments – including a drum and fife band!

Other times we worked with the Royal Engineers making up roads, laying railway tracks and water mains. This was the origin of the old army saying 'The bees do the work and the bees make the honey, but the Queens do the work and the REs draw the money!' I remember on one occasion I was on a wagon loaded with chalk for road mending and in the pouring rain the brakes failed and the poor old horse slipped on the slope and went down. The horse stopped the wagon, but the poor thing was rather badly cut. Almost everything was moved by horse wagon then.

It seems odd that we should have gone through all this with men dying every day a few miles away but we had to be kept fit and active I suppose, which is why we also played sports, particularly football. I played in many inter-platoon tournaments, and in the Brigade Sports held at Picquigny in May 1916 I managed to come in second in the 1 mile race and second in the high jump, winning 20 francs in each event. These sports took place during the last few days before we returned to the front line to prepare for the first Battle of the Somme. I remember I treated some of my pals with the money I'd won, but though I didn't know it, this was to be the last occasion I was ever going to be able to compete in sports.

We were at Picquigny, where we'd been given about two weeks rest after being at the front for eight months. It was a pleasant enough place, not far from Amiens. It was such a pleasure to see English girls – nurses – the first we'd seen for eight months. But all good things come to an end and we were soon boarding a train for Mericourt. From there we marched to Suzanne, a deserted derelict village just behind our front line. The weather, if I remember rightly, was good but the sandbags along our parapet on the front line were green and slimy as a result of mustard gas used by the Germans sometime before we arrived.

For the next few weeks things stayed fairly quiet but all the time preparations for the Somme battles were going on. Over the last ten days of June our artillery shelled the German lines day and night but we heard hardly a sound from the Germans. It was a massive bombardment but the Germans knew quite well that the attack was coming and they were fully prepared for it, a fact not known to us ordinary soldiers or, one would assume, to the top brass. We were led to believe that the German wire and defences would have been destroyed by the time we made our attack.

On Thursday 29 July 1916 we took up our positions in what were known as the assembly trenches. We were ready to go, but at the very last moment orders came through that the attack had been put off for forty-eight hours. We never knew why, but the weather turned foul and we had to stick in the trenches, packed together in the pouring rain with no cover at all. Two days later on Saturday July 1, at 7.30 in the morning, zero hour arrived. The weather had turned fine and warm, the trench ladders were in place and, on the blast of whistles and after wishing our chums the best of luck, we went up and over into no man's land where, under normal circumstances, you wouldn't have dared set foot in daylight. It wasn't terrifying at that moment, as many people today imagine it must have been, because we had been told again and again that this battle would be no battle at all. It would be a walk-over. There would be no opposition because we had bombed and shelled the German trenches into oblivion.

We had been drilled to go over in what was called star formation – in other words, the four sections of each platoon formed the four points of the star. Then, as we neared the German line, we were to spread out in extended order, that is into a long, straightish line. I was a bomber – that meant I was carrying 250 rounds of rifle ammunition, 7 Mills bombs strapped to my chest and 7 more strapped to my back. I was also carrying a rifle with bayonet fixed, and a pick and shovel. The idea of the pick and shovel was that we would need to square up the German trenches after we'd taken them. I was in the third wave of men who went over and I think I got about half-way to the German front trench.

To be as precise as possible I ought to say that I went over the top at a place called Carnoy. Our objective – and objectives were always explained to the men very precisely – was Montauban but, as it turned out, only a handful, if any, of the men in my battalion were to reach their objective. What we didn't know as we set off across no man's land that day, but were soon to discover, was that the Germans had been sheltering from our bombardment in complete safety in concrete dug-outs 30 ft down beneath their trenches. As soon as our attack started they came up out of these concrete dug-outs unharmed and ready for us. They came at us with what must have been dozens, perhaps even hundreds, of machine-guns as well as artillery fire. We were simply mown down. What made matters worse was that our field guns were using what was known as a creeping barrage for the first time. This meant firing over our heads but at the same time making sure that the shells landed just ahead of us among the Germans. I suspect that in the confusion a great many of our lads were actually killed and injured by our own artillery. Instead of it being a walk-over we were slaughtered. Something like 20,000 soldiers of Kitchener's great volunteer army were killed or wounded on that one day.

I can remember stumbling and tottering forward under the weight of all my bombs and equipment while all around me was the indescribable noise of shells bursting – you could feel the blast and hear and feel the red-hot jagged bits of metal swishing past you at every angle and height. I don't know how long I managed to keep going forward once I was up out of the trench, but I suppose I was always expecting to be hit, yet hoping against hope that somehow I wouldn't be. I couldn't turn back and, like all the men, I hoped that when I was hit it wouldn't be too bad. Moments later I was bowled right over by a hail of machine-gun bullets that completely shattered my right leg below the knee. All the time as I'd gone forward I'd seen flashes from machine-guns and rifles ahead of me on the ridge of the German trenches but I don't know which one hit me. I just felt a terrific thump, my leg gave way and I was down. There was no pain and I had the sense and the presence of mind to get rid of my bombs and to crawl into the nearest shell hole. Then, during the few moments that I remained conscious, I looked around and saw that the ground as far as I could see was covered with lads in khaki. The German barbed wire immediately in front of their trenches hadn't even been cut by our artillery and there were British soldiers dead all over it, hanging there and, of course, blocking the progress of the tiny number who made it that far without being hit. Those who did get that far found that the uncut wire and the bodies already lying tangled in it slowed them down long enough for the German gunners to make absolutely sure of them. And remember, the distance we'd been asked to cross between our trench and theirs was not more than a couple of hundred yards.

Wherever you looked there were dead soldiers in khaki, others were obviously dying, their life's blood leaking quickly away into the ground. Some were silent, others screamed in agony and terror. I saw that the ground everywhere was being spattered with shrapnel, high explosive and machine-gun bullets. It was virtually impossible not to get hit and the noise of it all was deafening, but I soon lost all awareness of what was happening because I was losing a lot of blood. I lay where I had fallen all through that long day – about fourteen hours in all, during which I regained consciousness only now and then. I was very lucky – just as I'd been lucky not to get killed in the first place like most of my friends – because as dusk fell I recovered consciousness for a moment, just as a young lad from the Royal Army Medical Corps came by looking for wounded. These chaps were always very brave, but they'd had to wait until things quietened down a little before they moved out over no man's land looking for wounded. I think he must have seen me move a little or I may have spoken to him. Anyway he came over and asked if I could walk. I tried to stand but fainted, so with the aid of one of his comrades he carried me back – and we were still under fire remember – to our front line where I discovered that I was just one of thousands lying waiting to be removed to a casualty clearing station.

A great many died before getting there and many others were killed as they lay on their stretchers by shell fire or stray bullets. Thousands lost one or more limbs or their sight or their hands. Most of my friends were killed in that first half-hour. Of the fifteen men in my section, two came back.

Eventually, after several hours, I was placed on a stretcher and carried into a field dressing station where my leg was given some emergency treatment before I was placed in an ambulance that took me to hospital in Amiens. There were no beds for us so we were just lined up on stretchers.

Some time later we were given a wash and our wounds were freshly dressed. Still wearing our filthy khaki uniforms we spent five days on stretchers, cared for by nuns who were very kind. They fed us and did all they could to ease our pain. Many of the lads were in great pain and many died, but I survived this and after a few days was put on a hospital barge and towed down the River Somme to hospital in Abbeville. This was the first time I'd been in a bed for over a year and it felt like heaven after all those months of active service living under such squalid conditions.

At Abbeville we were given fresh underwear and new uniforms and then we were taken by train to what was known as the No. 3 Canadian Hospital in Boulogne. The train actually took us to the docks to board a hospital ship, but when we got there the ship was full so we were taken back to the hospital where we stayed for three days. By then it was eight days from the time we'd left the battlefield. I wasn't feeling too bad by now, although my leg was a bit painful and I could not put my foot on the floor.

I think it was on the evening of Sunday 9 July when we were taken back down to the docks at Boulogne for another attempt to get us on a hospital ship. This time we were lucky and we boarded the *Western Australia*. We sailed later in the evening and after seventeen hours docked at Southampton. It took such a long time because we were constantly dodging German U-boats. While on board a label was stuck on me saying that I was to go to London, but the hospital train waiting at Southampton was actually bound for Aberdeen, as I discovered later. Because I wasn't as badly wounded as many of the men I was given one of the top bunks on the train.

We left Southampton at about lunch time and when we stopped at Basingstoke I thought, 'This looks like we're going to London', but the next stop was at Snow Hill, Birmingham, and I suddenly realized I hadn't a clue where we were going. By 11 July, a Tuesday, we were in Aberdeen and I had been away from the front for eleven days. I chuckled at the thought that here in Scotland I was actually further from home than I'd ever been in France. Anyway, we were taken to the Old Mill Military Hospital, and I was to remain here, mostly in bed, for the next six months.

During all the travelling the wound in my leg had become infected with gangrene and, after suffering great pain and many operations carried out to try to save it, my right leg had to be amputated high above the knee. By this time I was almost a skeleton and when I was taken to the operating theatre for the umpteenth time I told the surgeon (a Captain Mitchell as I recall) that if he was going to take my leg off he could take it off at the neck as I'd had enough. This happened on 20 September 1916 and of course it meant that my war service was over for ever.

After the leg had been amputated and most of the pain had gone I was able to move in bed. This was a great relief because for almost three months prior to the operation which removed my leg I had been unable to move at all as the leg was kept in plaster from top to bottom, and afterwards in a Thomas splint with a weight on the end, which meant I just had to lie on my back with bed sores as big as saucers. With my leg gone I gradually regained my strength and after a few more weeks I was able to get out of bed. The first time I got out I had the strangest feeling – it was as if I was going to float up and up and up! When I reached my full height, 6 ft, I just collapsed and that was my lot for the day! But as the days wore on I made progress and was soon able to ride around in a wheelchair. Like most amputees, I sometimes tried to put down the foot that wasn't there. I couldn't help it – the problem was that although the leg had gone I could still feel my toes tingling as I can to this day.

Towards the end of 1916 I was sent to Dr Gray's Hospital in Elgin to convalesce. I remember that during my first days here the other lads used to take me out in an old-fashioned bath chair and once they pushed the bath chair with me in it into an ornamental pond in Cooper's Park! The water wasn't too deep, and I was soon rescued. On the way back to the hospital they pushed me into a pub and I was well received by the patrons who had a whip round for my benefit. After this experience I asked the matron for crutches and was given a pair of the old broom-handle kind. With practice I soon got used to them and got around quite well, although the first time I tried to go down the front steps at the hospital I fell down most of them!

It was universally agreed among all the wounded I met at Elgin and Aberdeen that we were marvellously looked after – we wanted for nothing and apart from those first three months when I suffered acutely, I enjoyed my hospital days. The Scottish people were very kind and generous too – most places of entertainment in the area were free to us and the golf course in Elgin was available if we wanted to play. We had no trouble getting a round of golf with the local girls, although I had to balance on one leg when hitting the ball. With my crutches I got round and could play a fair game. Just before my twenty-first birthday it was decided that I should be sent to a hospital closer to my home in Woking. I was sad to go as I'd made many friends in Elgin.

In spite of the length of time that had passed since my operation my stump had still not healed and it was thought that I would have to undergo another operation. Fortunately, however, I was transferred to a VAD Hospital called Beechcroft where the matron found an ointment which healed the wound and a further operation was avoided.

It was April 1917 when I arrived back at my home in Woking. After a few weeks leave which I spent with my parents and with friends at Salisbury I was admitted to Roehampton Hospital to be fitted with an artificial leg. By January 1918 I was on two legs again although one was made from willow, as all artificial legs were in those days, and it weighed about 9 lb – a considerable weight to carry around.

At this time I began to wonder what on earth I would do with the rest of my life. I didn't want to go back to the ironmonger's trade, although I'd been an apprentice at it from 1910 till 1914. I was discharged from the army in February 1918 after almost two years in hospital and I found civilian life very difficult at first. This was partly because I just wasn't used to it and partly because I missed the wonderful companionship of army friends.

I spent six months at the Regent Street Polytechnic in London on an engineering course and while I was there I lived in Hanover Square. I don't think I could quite afford to live there now! Anyway we were actually staying in a house owned by Vesta Tilley, the actress. She took a great interest in helping the war disabled, and since that time I've always been fond of saying that I once slept in Vesta Tilley's bed!

The loss of my leg never really interfered with the rest of my life. After some years in engineering I got a job as a schools' inspector and did that for thirty-six years until my retirement at sixty-five. Since then I've had more than thirty years of happy retirement and in my life I've had two wives – both real good 'uns! For years I swam regularly in the rivers and ponds around Woking – often with one of my dogs – and I was always reckoned to be the best one-legged wicket-keeper in Woking!

In those days officers and men were a different species. The line of social class was very rigidly drawn, but today when I'm invited to army occasions and dinners I'm always invited to sit at the top table with the officers! How the world has changed.

CHAPTER TWO

RICHARD HAWKINS

Richard Hawkins is ninety-seven. A slight figure, alert and with eyes that still sparkle and a firm handshake, he is troubled only by arthritis in his legs and hands. He still wears the crisp, military moustache he wore more than seventy-five years ago when he set off for Colchester Barracks to join up in 1914, right at the start of the Great War. Richard was born in Chelmsford, Essex on 8 March 1895. His father, a noted amateur entertainer and practical joker, was chief accountant at the electrical manufacturer's Crompton & Co. After the war, Richard was to spend more than forty-six years working in the same industry, but for Belling & Co. Richard's earliest memories are of the horses pulling carts and carriages through what was then an old market town many miles from London. He started work as an apprentice at the long-vanished engineering firm of Hofmanns and then made plans to emigrate to Canada. He was ready to go when war broke out.

I said straight away that I would have to leave and join up. But that was the thing then. You didn't think about it. It was simply automatic. Thousands and thousands of young men were trying to join up. But the boss at the company for which I was working was furious when he heard. He called me an ungrateful so and so. And, as I recall, his three sons never went near the war.

Then one day, quite determined, I set off from Chelmsford for London. I thought that would be the obvious place to join up. I'd been in the King Edward VI Grammar School cadet corps – in fact, I had been a sergeant and was a prize-winning shot – so I thought I'd have no trouble.

But London was quite simply flooded with young men trying to do exactly the same thing. It was incredible. The streets were full of us, all with just one aim. And wherever we went the army couldn't cope. They were too busy they said. I tried absolutely everywhere and eventually got accepted at a public schools' battalion – the Royal Fusiliers. I can remember the grey, drizzling morning when I took the King's shilling. It was at St Martins in the Fields.

I was given a few days leave and told to join up at Hounslow Barracks, but meanwhile I met a governor of the grammar school in Chelmsford who suggested I go to Colchester to meet his son-in-law, Lt.-Col. Carr. I set off on a borrowed motor bike and, after a chat, Col. Carr gave me a note to someone he knew at the War Office. I went down there on Sunday, my particulars were taken down and I was told to go to Hounslow. I was also given £30 to buy a uniform and a Webley revolver which cost, I believe, £3. After a couple of days at Hounslow I got orders to return to Colchester.

By the time I got back to Essex I'd met up with two regular soldiers, but we were given a pretty cold reception. When we arrived the colonel shouted to another officer, 'Some more of these damned young officers have arrived.'

'Tell them to go away,' came the reply!

I hadn't a clue what to do and it's hard to imagine now just how chaotic it all was. Col. Carr's quartermaster saw a vast number of civilians coming up North Hill in Colchester. They told him they were the Middlesex and he replied, 'Oh no you're not. You're the 11th Service Battalion of the Royal Fusiliers.' The Stock Exchange (10th Battalion) had a Rothschild as cook and he was the only one with a uniform! That's how the 11th Service Battalion of the Royal Fusiliers – my battalion – was formed.

Kitchener's Army – the first hundred thousand – was officered entirely by people like me. At the age of nineteen I was given the 16th platoon, forty men. All we knew how to do was shoot and drill. We were in the 18th division, the 54th brigade, with the seventh Bedfordshire, the sixth Northamptonshire and the 11th Royal Fusiliers. Our training at Colchester seemed to consist entirely of running up North Hill every morning!

Early in 1915 we were handed over to General Sir Ivor Maxse. He was known as the finest training general in the British Army. He managed to transform us until we thought we were the best battalion in the British Army. In fact, we were so full of ourselves that I really think we were heartily disliked by the rest of the army. And quite right too!

Maxse survived the war and lived into his nineties. I think he ran an apple orchard eventually. If an apple ever fell off a tree without his permission I'm convinced he'd have told it off!

A day I remember particularly well was 1 July 1916 – the Battle of the Somme. It was a nice day, warm, but misty early on. Every man had a packet of Woodbines in his pocket. Our guns plastered the other side till the Germans went down into their 30 ft deep dug-outs. Then off we went. We were lucky and met little opposition, believe it or not. It really is true that we could have walked straight to Berlin. It was all over by lunch-time – for us. The problem was on both our flanks where the fighting was ferocious. That's where they got the worst of it. And all the time General Maxse – he was only 5 ft 6 in tall and his equerry was 6 ft 3 in – watched the battle through his field-glasses. I remember he came to see us. 'Good morning gentlemen,' he said. 'Damned good show!' But having made us relax by saying that, he then asked us the following question: 'Where would you expect to find a British officer in the biggest battle ever?' Dead silence! 'Walking about on the skyline looking for souvenirs!' He'd caught us fair and square because that's exactly what we'd been doing. That was typical of him.

He'd lift you up and then dash you down, but I've still got the German helmet I picked up.

Prior to going out to the front we'd had only about six months training. And I can still remember crossing the English Channel. It was night. The troops always crossed at night and we were escorted on either side by destroyers because the sea was full of enemy submarines. From Ostrohove Camp we gradually moved up to the front and in due course took over a stretch of trench at Fricourt. We took it over from the Oxfordshire and Bucks. I remember that trench well. It was exactly 30 yards – no more – from the nearest enemy trench. Just before we got there the whole of that trench had been successfully mined and blown up by German engineers. We'd lost a lot of men. The Germans had dug tunnels out from their side and under our unsuspecting troops. Then they filled the tunnel with explosive and up went all our men. It was always a sort of cat and mouse game. When we took over the trench we had a brilliant Australian engineer with us who dug special tunnels out toward the Germans. He filled these with explosive in such a way that they produced a flat explosion. The idea – and it worked well – was to destroy the enemy's tunnelling. We gradually got command of the situation and the Germans gave up trying their tunnels against us. But for a long time we were effectively sitting on a minefield.

A common tactic on both sides at this time was deliberately to produce a shell crater between our trench and the enemy. We would then try to dig out to the edge of the crater before the Germans could reach their side of the same crater. Some of these craters were 30 ft deep and we had to crawl out to check them. If a crater had what we called a lip we would get a man to crawl out to the lip so he could lob bombs over the crater at the enemy. It was a messy, bloody awful kind of warfare.

It was made messier by the French who'd been there before us. They didn't bother to remove their dead so when a shell came over it used to blow bits of the dead lying in no man's land all over the living still in the trenches. Sometimes a shell would bury those it had killed and then, a few weeks later, another shell would explode in the same place and blow the dead and buried all over the place. By that time the bodies were badly decayed or half eaten by rats. It was so terrible. It was indescribable.

And, of course, the rats grew fat on the dead. But they were never satisfied with that. They would take the chocolate from your pockets at night if you weren't careful. And they were as big as young rabbits. They would attack if you cornered them. But what you have to try to imagine everywhere is the smell of the dead and the smell of cordite, the dead and the half dead everywhere, the muck, the filth, the half buried. So many were killed and buried by the shells. So many were never found.

In the trenches we were always nervous because the Germans, even when they were not digging under us, tried to persuade us that they were. They would dig out towards us and then rig up a pick on the end of a string. When the string was pulled it would sound like digging and of course we were always listening for the diggers. You had to learn the difference between genuine digging and the fake kind designed to keep us on edge. Sometimes of course they would use fake digging noises to make us think they were still digging when, in fact, they had reached the stage where they were carrying the explosive into the tunnel beneath us.

One of the big problems was that they had more artillery than we did. This could lead to some really tricky situations. On one occasion we were getting badly strafed. We thought we were about to be attacked so we asked our battery to fire at the Germans. They rang us and said they were rationed to forty rounds per gun per week. This was Wednesday and they were re-supplied on Sunday. 'You can have the lot now and then nothing till Sunday,' they said. The Germans had a thing called a *Minnenwerfer*. You could hear and see it coming so at least you had time to react! The shells it fired were the size of a 5 gallon oil drum and they were filled with bits of rusty metal that would fly in all directions when the thing exploded. Our machine-gun was bloody useless. We didn't want it because it only attracted artillery fire.

I did get leave now and then, as we all did, and I remember I used to get off the train in London and go straight to Jermyn Street to the Turkish Bath. Then I'd have lunch with my mother at the Trocadero.

I was in France, in the trenches, for a total of nineteen months. Apart from the Somme I fought at Trones Wood, Thiepval and Miraumont, or Boom Ravine as it was known.

I was hit at Boom Ravine and all my original friends and most of the men had been killed or wounded by then. I suppose I was one of the last of the original hundred thousand – Kitchener's Army – who volunteered in 1914. That was the cream of the army, but most had gone, dead or wounded, by the time of Boom Ravine.

I know it sounds strange but even amid the slaughter there was some humour. I remember, for example, at Thiepval, an officer had the end of his John Thomas shot off – quite literally, I'm not kidding! A machine-gun swung round and just caught him. After that he was always being asked at dinner and in the mess if it was still working!

At Thiepval the Germans resisted all our attacks. An Irish brigade had gone in before us and not one man was ever seen again. It was 25 September 1916 when we were sent in. I remember what we were told. 'The 14th Wertemburgers have resisted all attacks, but tomorrow the 18th division (that was us) will take it.' That's what we were told – and we did it. My battalion had to keep one trench down with artillery fire. Then we were told to cross no man's land and go down the German dug-outs. We were not to throw bombs, we were to go in there and fight them hand to hand.

Mind you, it's not true that the senior officers stayed out of the fighting. Brigadier Maxwell is a good example of one type of commanding officer. He arrived on the night before the Battle of the Somme to take his command and be in the battle, but he wasn't due to take over for another day by which time we would have been leaving. He simply felt he had to take part in the battle. Eventually he got shot in the bottom while walking across the top of a trench in full view of the enemy. The men adored him.

After the Somme we found ourselves in an area called Happy Valley. Here the trenches were filled – absolutely filled – with the bodies of the dead. All we could do was walk over them. There were so many it was impossible to avoid them. They were all that remained of the brigade that had been in the trench before us. They'd all died. Even though I was hardened to the sight of the dead by then, it was still a terrible shock to see it. They'd been attempting to clear a wood some 300 yards away. They failed completely. Whether we were just luckier or what I don't know, but we went into that wood, lined out across it and cleared it with few losses.

I was wounded at Boom Ravine just before the big retreat across the Hindenburg Line. It started on 17 February 1917. It had been freezing for weeks, so cold that spilled mustard on the floor of the hut would freeze in minutes. We moved up in the middle of the night to a place known as Oxford Circus. We formed up just in front of a gulley. From here a sunken road known as The Ravine ran up to the main ravine, or Boom Ravine as we called it. Boom Ravine was our objective. Anyway the junction of the sunken road with the gulley was known as Oxford Circus. It was absolutely pitch black I remember and everywhere knee-deep in mud and filth. The ground was churned up and there were shell holes everywhere. All the time as we moved up and while we waited we were swept by machine-gun and rifle fire – every yard of the journey. However, we were in position by, I think, 4.45 a.m. There were only two ways up to the forming-up place – one via the duck-boards, the other via a trench that I think was known as Cornwall Trench. Both routes were badly congested and it was very difficult to move into position in the pitch darkness.

For at least three weeks it had been freezing and on this night it began to thaw in a big way. As a result the ground was quite indescribable and all night long we were plastered by artillery fire. The Germans had obviously got to know of the coming attack. They knew our zero hour. We had a lot of casualties even as we gathered in the dark at Oxford Circus. I went round the line with some rum at 5.30 a.m. and I gave what remained of my company a good tot and had a chat to them. Each man received 1/8 of a pint a day and I really believe that, more than anything else, it was the rum that got most of us through. It used to go right down to your boots. The rum ration in the British Army stopped soon after the war ended, but it was a stronger rum than any I've had since. I believe that it was actually old Navy rum.

There wasn't a level bit of ground for miles. We waded through mud and slime and fell into shell holes and some of these were between 10 and 30 ft deep. The ground had been pounded into an extraordinary state. Mud and ice, bodies and craters were everywhere .

It was, I suppose, about 6 a.m. by the time I'd finished going round with the rum and chatting to the men. They were just about all right in terms of morale and on the whole we hadn't had so many casualties. I thought I would establish my HQ on the side of the ravine that led to Boom Ravine. So at about 6.20 I went up through the filth and muck to the top of the ravine – it was about 25 or perhaps 30 ft high. I climbed up with my servant, the company sergeant major, a signaller and a runner. Somehow we got to the top. I'd explained to my company that I'd be on the right hand edge. I could just see my watch and it was 6.25 by now and unfortunately still dark. And all the time it was thawing and the mud was getting worse. At 6.28 the biggest barrage imaginable suddenly opened on us. Clearly the Hun had discovered when the battle was to begin. Dear old Collis Sands, the commander of B Company turned up at my side. He said to me 'I think this is going to be a pretty awful show.' I agreed and said I thought I would get a rifle. I thought I'd need one. I got one from a dead man and then waited the last couple of minutes till zero hour – 6.30. At exactly 6.30 our barrage opened up with a blinding flash behind us, but unfortunately we were still bogged down by the German barrage. I said again to Collis Sands that this was going to be a very dirty fight and he agreed. He also told me that he didn't know where exactly his company had got to. Then as we stood waiting, there was a blinding flash from behind us on the opposite side of the ravine. Poor Collis Sands was hit and went down immediately and then something hit me in the shoulder and spun me round. I felt like I'd been kicked by a mule and fell down the deep ravine. I crashed into the barbed wire at the bottom. I think that knocked me out for a bit because the next thing I knew it was just about light.

I was out of it for a while and then I remember hearing a cockney voice saying 'God, it's Captain Hawkins. He's dead.'

'No I'm not,' I said, 'but I soon will be if you don't get me out of here.'

They all called me Henry after the musical hall character. I discovered later that my fellow officer, Collis Sands, a dear chap, had been killed instantly as he stood by my side.

The stretcher-bearers took me back to our lines and a doctor ordered me into a very deep German dug-out we'd taken. It was really very comfortable compared to the awful trenches we normally had. The Germans were terribly methodical at building them deep and very secure.

The doctor tried to get four captured German soldiers to carry my stretcher. One refused to do it – in fact the doctor had to kick this young officer in the bottom to get him to move. That was one of the funniest things I ever saw. The doctor ran after that young officer launching great kicks at him every few yards, but mostly missing and the two of them slipping and falling continually in the mud as they ran. Eventually the young German gave in and picked up his corner of my stretcher, but I knew they'd tip me into a shell hole as soon as the doctor was out of sight so I hopped off and walked. By this stage I was in a hell of a state. I'd lost an awful lot of blood and there was frozen water in my boots. When I got to the

casualty clearing station I asked for a hot-water bottle – I was afraid
I'd lose my feet with frost-bite – and miraculously they managed to
find me one. I decided that I'd waited a long time for a decent
wound and having got one I didn't want to lose my feet into the
bargain!

They used neat ether to anaesthetize us in those days – the taste
was absolutely disgusting. I found out later that the piece of
shrapnel that hit me had missed an artery by $1/8$ in. If it had hit the
artery I would have been dead in a couple of seconds.

The most extraordinary thing about being in the trenches was
how you came simply to accept death. I can remember on several
occasions going to pick up a man, lifting his leg and having it come
off in my hand.

It is nonsense too when you hear people saying that Field
Marshal Haig sent thousands to their deaths. Do you think he
wanted them to die? Something had to be done. Belgium had
gone. France had nearly gone. We'd lost most of our regular army
at Mons. We had to move at the Somme, even though it meant
terrible losses. We had to attack. If we hadn't the French would
have soon surrendered and the Kaiser would have overrun us.

King George V gave me my medal. I remember the flunky
telling me to take twelve paces, turn left, take ten paces, then stop,
then his majesty would pin the medal on me. I then had to take
two steps back and leave. The whole thing was totally confusing.
All I remember about the king was that he was wearing field boots.

I think I was awarded my MC for killing a German soldier. Just
one. I'd been walking along a trench at Thiepval when, at a corner, I
walked straight into a German officer. He whipped out his Luger, but
I was slightly quicker on the draw and I shot him. It was as simple as
that. One of us was going to die and I didn't want it to be me.

We used to sleep on raised platforms half-way up the sides of the
trenches. All the men did about six days on and six days off – six in
the trenches and then six back at a village behind the lines. That
was fairly civilized because we were living in people's houses.

Back in London I eventually went to convalesce at a house at Stanhope Gate owned by a Mrs Holdsworth, a relative of Lady Apsley. We were looked after like kings. She was an absolutely marvellous woman. In 1919 I was demobbed all by myself at Crystal Palace and I went back to my life in Chelmsford. I worked on the sales side at Bellings and eventually became sales director. I was there for fifty-six years in total.

In all I don't think I killed many Germans, but we were told that if we took prisoners we'd have to feed them and then after the war they'd produce lots of little Germans our children would eventually have to fight.

Every year after the war ended my comrades and I – the survivors – had a dinner. That lasted for a long time and our battalion flag, or the shreds of it that remain, hangs to this day in St Paul's Cathedral.

CHAPTER THREE

FRED DIXON

Fred Dixon always thinks of Christmas when he thinks of the Great War: Christmas 1914 he was in England; Christmas 1915 in France on the Somme: Christmas 1916 in Italy on the Piave; Christmas 1918 in Belgium at the Meuse and Christmas 1919 on the Rhine in occupied Germany. Now ninety-six, he joined up on 20 October 1914. He was eighteen and before military service he'd been apprenticed to the stationery trade. Yet even before the great sadnesses of the war he had faced troubles at home with great equanimity, as he remembered when I met him in Elstead near Godalming, Surrey, where he lives quietly today.

My father had two stationery shops in Westcott which failed so we moved to Woking, but the move had serious consequences for me. At Westcott I had been selected by the village headmaster to work for a scholarship to Dorking High School and we left before I could sit the exam. My sister was already at the county school for girls at Redhill. In my new school I was told that I could not take a scholarship exam until I had been there two years and by then I would have been too old anyway so I missed my chance. I left school at fourteen but I knew my parents needed my wages anyway as my father's businesses had failed.

My first job was as a paper-boy employed by W.H. Smith on Woking Station. I had to get up at 5.30 to be there for 6 a.m. My round was finished by 8.15 and I then had breakfast before returning to the station by 9 a.m. when I took charge of one of the bookstalls on the platform. There was no future in the job so I left after a few months and got a job as an office boy with a firm of builders and hot-water engineers in Woking. My hours were 8 a.m. to 8 p.m. and my wages 5s. a week. That was another dead-end job so I left after a short while and started a three-year apprenticeship to the retail stationery trade. Most days I worked from 8 a.m. to 8.30 p.m. or from 8 a.m. to 10 p.m.! I had to ask for the boss's permission to go to night-school even though his son went off every day as a fee-paying pupil to the school I'd hoped to enter on a scholarship. I felt no loyalty to my employer when war came in 1914. I'd felt exploited and although by joining up I was swapping one form of servitude for another, at least in the army I would be treated as a man and not as a boy.

It's very difficult now to imagine what the world was like in those days – how people lived and the kind of social class system that existed and the effects it had on the way people behaved toward each other.

In my home we had toys, but we were not allowed to play with them on Sundays and during the long winter evenings everything outside was dark and totally silent. There were no street lamps in the village so we stayed indoors and amused ourselves. We played endless games of ludo, snakes and ladders and happy families. Playing-cards were forbidden because they were considered to be the first step on the gambling road to hell. We played our games by the light of an oil lamp and we went to bed by candle-light. Everyone did. Radio was non-existent until after the Great War and, of course, there was no television until after the second war. Beer was cheap and strong and drunkenness was rife.

I remember seeing my first film at the town hall in Dorking in 1902. Parts of the film terrified me and I hid under my chair. In

Woking every Saturday night you would see the poor people waiting outside all the butchers' shops for sixpenny joints that the butcher knew he could not keep till Monday because, of course, there was no refrigeration. Working men had to work until they dropped for there were almost no pensions. If you were ill and had no money you got no help at all from the state. Even in the church – perhaps especially in the church – class distinctions were strictly adhered to. The patron's family sat in the chancel behind the choir stalls, the gentry occupied the centre block of pews in the nave, and the tradespeople and their families sat on the north side where the cold winds blew through ventilators at floor level. Domestic servants and land workers sat in the pews at the back behind the font.

My apprenticeship was part of this whole system so I didn't feel too bad when I broke it after two years to train with the 6th Dragoons who were then stationed in Dorking. We were sent to Canterbury to be trained to ride at the cavalry school and we learned sword drill and musketry. I was quite a reasonable horseman.

Perhaps I should explain why I joined up rather than waiting to be conscripted. Apart from disliking my apprenticeship it really all goes back to my childhood, to about 1900, in fact. When I was four my mother took me in a wooden mail cart to see the Surrey Yeomanry who were camping under the shadow of the North Downs about two miles from Dorking. I loved the sight of the horses and the men in their khaki uniforms with red facings. They had been given the nickname Cubitt's Robins after Colonel the Honorable Guy Cubitt who commanded the regiment for a number of years before the First World War.

Each summer a troop or perhaps a squadron would pass along the main Dorking to Guildford Road through Westcott, the little village where I lived. I watched them, loving the white head ropes, the glorious horses, the shining bits, stirrups and spurs. When war came in 1914 I knew it wouldn't be over by Christmas and I thought it would be better to join the regiment of my choice rather than wait to be called up into a regiment I might not wish to join. So I went along and signed up for the Surrey Yeomanry. My mother thought I'd made the right decision. Many of my friends in nearby Woking joined the 7th Battalion, The Queen's, and most were killed at Carnoy on the first day of the Battle of the Somme, 1 July. I was to be rather lucky on that occasion because although temporarily dismounted we did not enter the front line at La Boisselle until 4 July when the first blood-bath had lessened a little.

Our training mainly consisted of an attempt to impress on us that we were a sub-human breed. If they set out to break our hearts and did not succeed it was not for want of trying. We got up at 5 a.m. and ran 4 miles. Then back at the stables Sergeant Jock Simpson would shout, 'Now then you bloody bastards.' He then made us muck out with our hands – we even had to take wet straw outside for it to dry. Grooming, wisping and feeding followed and then we could have our own breakfast. We couldn't wash our hands first – it simply wasn't allowed – and we had to have eaten, dressed, saddled and mounted for parade in forty-five minutes.

Then we had one hour in the riding school, often without stirrups. We were soundly abused most of the time, but our major got his come-uppance one day when he swore at a soldier from the Royal Canadian Dragoons. The major, 'Jackie' Lloyd, called the Canadian a 'bloody bastard' so the Canadian drew his sword and ran his horse at the major before chasing him across the polo ground!

Grooming was always done strictly to order and even patting our horses had to be done by numbers. The order would be given to 'Make much of your horses'. And we were frequently reminded that our horses were valuable. A horse cost £50 but you could get a man for a shilling. (I should mention that before I joined up I had obtained my crossed flags as a signaller in the Church Lads Brigade, part of a cadet battalion. I was proficient in semaphore, morse, flags and buzzer.)

Anyway, training complete, I found myself, at nineteen, a private in the Surrey Yeomanry in Egypt on the Western Front fighting Sennusi arabs. It was 1915. Here on one occasion I remember a rather funny incident when I had to use two pocket handkerchiefs to semaphore as I stood in my stirrups. Fighting in North Africa was no preparation for fighting in France and Belgium, but in 1916 we were ordered back to France, to the Somme where thousands and thousands were gathering for that most terrible battle. We got there just in time for 1 July when it began. The guns had been pounding the German positions for a full week and the air and the earth were still shaking when we arrived and began our preparations.

I was in the forward trench when the Lochnager Mine was detonated. It was about 7.30 on 1 July and the explosion occurred out in front of our trench and just in front of the German front line. The crater caused by the Lochnager Mine was 300 ft wide and almost 90 ft deep. I discovered afterwards that 27 tons of explosives went into that mine and it is still said to be the biggest hole ever made by man in anger. We went out under fire to the crater and used it to take cover from German fire. I remember the ground was absolutely littered with bodies. A tunnel was dug from the front line trench to the crater to keep our troops supplied. I was an ammunition carrier to the Hotchkiss gun team situated on our front line directly facing the crater. I was still a private in the Surrey Yeomanry (Cavalry) at this time and ammunition carrying was the sort of auxiliary duty we had to carry out. I was given a place at the end of the front line trench right where the Lochnager Mine went up. I recall one incident particularly clearly from this time. We had a very deep dug-out behind us and one day Major Bonsor, our commanding officer, came up from the dug-out only to hear a bullet whisper inches past his head. I think a sniper at the nearby village of La Boisselle had spotted the movement of the woollen scarf he kept on his head like a hat. He simply turned to me and, cool as you please, said; 'That was a near one, Dixon.' What could I do but agree?

As a point of interest I should say that during 1991 a farmer stumbled across that deep dug-out which had survived intact. He was ploughing when his machine disappeared into an 18 ft hole. I was told the position of the rediscovered dug-out and it was undoubtedly the one where Major Bonsor and I had had that exchange.

The Battle of the Somme lasted until 13 November, well into one of the coldest winters there had been for something like fifty years. We were issued with special sheepskin topcoats.

Our week-long barrage at the Somme had done no good at all because the Germans were too well dug in. The shells didn't really hurt them so when our men began to move forward the Germans popped up and began to mow them down. We'd been told it would be a walk-over – or rather the poor bloody infantry had been told that it would. And by this time I'd been transferred to the infantry.

It occurs to me that many people don't fully realize from the published figures the extent of our casualties during the Somme. On 1 July 20,000 men were killed. If you walk from Guildford High Street to the main roundabout just west of Farnham – a distance of 11⅓ miles – you must imagine that a man was killed for every yard you walked, and killed in just one day. On the same day 37,000 were wounded and of course many of those died of their wounds. By 13 November 415,000 had been killed or injured in that battle.

At Beaumont Hamel on the Somme the Newfoundland Regiment was almost wiped out. A week before the battle they were told by General Beauvoir de Lisle that the Allies outnumbered the Germans by about three to one. This was completely untrue. They were also told that a great victory now would be the beginning of the end of the war. The British front line was manned by the 2nd South Wales Borderers and the 1st Royal Inniskilling Fusiliers; the intermediary line was manned by the 1st King's Own Scottish Borderers and the 1st Border Regiment. The Newfoundlanders were in the rear.

On 1 July after a heavy bombardment the battle began. On some sections of the line that first rush was successful at the start, but at Beaumont Hamel it failed disastrously. The bombardment hadn't silenced the German guns, nor knocked out their front line, nor pulverized their wire. As a result the first attack by the South Wales Borderers and the Inniskillings as well as the second attack by the KOSBs and the Border Regiment were repulsed with terrible losses.

Uncertain about whether the German front line had been taken or not, Divisional HQ was debating an order to the Newfoundlanders to attack when it was reported that flares were going up above the German trenches. This was a German signal for artillery support, but by unhappy coincidence it was also a pre-arranged British signal that the German front line had been captured. The Newfoundlanders were therefore ordered to attack.

The two British forward lines were already crammed with wounded and survivors from the first two attacks so, instead of going over the top from the British front line, the Newfoundlanders were ordered into the open from their reserve line. This meant they were under machine-gun fire from 500 yards away. They were also carrying 66 lb packs – including sledge hammers and even paint for marking captured guns with the regimental insignia!

For the first 250 yards they trudged through gaps in the British wire and across plank bridges thrown over the two forward trenches. Once into no man's land and with the corpses from the previous attack blocking the gaps in the German wire the men began to fall in their hundreds. They plodded on without artillery support for the British guns had shifted to the German intermediary line thinking the forward trench had been taken. Forty minutes after the start not one Newfoundlander was left standing. Half the original 752 men were dead, most of the rest badly wounded. Sixty had taken refuge in shell holes. The wounded lay moaning and crying throughout that blazing hot July day not daring to move because of snipers. Only after darkness fell did stretcher parties dare go out to help. At the end of that day 91 per cent of the battalion had been killed or wounded. All the officers and 658 men.

Of the million or so British casualties on the Somme 70,000 simply disappeared – they were blown to pieces and buried under tons of mud and rubble.

The carnage here and elsewhere was terrible but you had to accept it. What else could you do?

In October 1917 we were ordered to Italy because the Italian line had been broken at Caporetto. After six days in what were little better than cattle trucks we reached Mantua and what I remember really well about that time are the lice. I scratched myself sore from ankle to waist. Men used to shave off their body hair to try to get rid of the damn things. I reported sick and only recovered when an orderly picked off every scab on my body with a pair of tweezers.

I nearly came unstuck in Italy when the Prince of Wales was due to pay us a visit. On the morning of the visit I was sent to our transport lines to collect, of all things, a bicycle. I was under direct observation by the Austrian gunners all the way along the road and across the fields. On the way back I had to carry the bicycle across a muddy field. Army bicycles were pretty heavy and although I was very fit from continual horse riding my muscles suddenly cramped and I was in such agony I just had to lie across the machine and listen as the Austrians started shelling and the splinters flew around me. Incredibly I wasn't even touched. We left Italy to return to France on 1 March 1918 and arrived at our base on 5 March. The German spring offensive was imminent.

I remember one amusing thing that happened at Dijon at around this time. A very kind old lady was dispensing coffee and rum from a jug and two very much younger girls were dispensing pills which they assured us would give extra power to our amorous exploits. Colonel Hayley Bell, father of Mary and grandfather of the actress, Hayley Mills, took the opportunity to swallow two!

I should say at this stage that signalmen like me were in a rather odd position in the war in some ways. Among the small number of signalmen in a cavalry squadron there is practically no promotion, especially when some are peacetime yeomen. When we were transferred to the infantry the position was different and I was offered promotion several times but I always refused. The reason was that I was part of a very closely knit group of Battalion Headquarters signallers. I would have lost all my friends had I accepted a stripe because I would probably have been transferred to take charge of the company signallers.

I was offered a commission in the Indian Cavalry and even filled in the application form. I'd been abroad for almost three years at the time and thought this was a chance to escape to something different. As it was, the Armistice came and all commissions were cancelled, but a friend of mine who'd applied a little earlier was accepted and found himself on his way to India when the Armistice came. He was later wounded so I considered I'd had a lucky escape.

On 28 September 1918 I was part of the advance at Ypres through the leading battalion by way of Shrapnel Corner and Hill 60. Once down the other side of the hill we had the Ypres–Comines Canal as our right flank. When night fell we signallers went forward to Kjortewilde and then suddenly, as we progressed, there came the sound of rattling harness. I thought they were ration mules but some of the chaps thought they were Germans and started firing in the direction of the sound, which was coming from a plank road behind us. This plank road ran through what had been the canal to an area on our right where, as yet, there had been no advance. We decided we could not place ourselves in such a tricky position so we retraced our steps until the plank road was in front of us. We also decided that a sentry should remain while the rest retired to a pillbox to try to get some sleep. I volunteered to be the sentry.

Ten minutes after being left alone I heard a noise so I challenged, but there was no answer. I tried again and got an indistinct reply which I did not understand. I walked forward with bayonet fixed, one up the spout and my finger on the trigger. I walked straight into a German. I don't know how I had the presence of mind to do it, but I made him drop his rifle and I forced his hands up with my bayonet. I walked around him and came across another German, and another and another – seven in all! I called for assistance and a lance corporal came and helped me take them to Battalion Headquarters where he reported the capture and was later decorated for it.

One of my saddest memories I suppose is of an incident that took place with some new arrivals, or A4 boys as they were known. There were about a dozen who'd just arrived from England and nobody seemed to be in charge of them. When I came across them they were running up and down the Ypres–Comines Canal bank like a lot of kids. I said to them, 'If you'll take my tip you'll cut that out. We are under observation here.' They just shouted back, 'Windy' at me, meaning I was afraid. I replied sharply, 'Yes I am. That's why I've been out so long.' And I showed them my 1915 medal ribbon. Anyway I wasn't going to argue so I said, 'You get on with it. I'm getting under cover.' I went into a nearby splinter-proof shelter and sat down. Three minutes later a 5.9 shell fell in the swampy bed of the canal outside. Seconds later a second shell fell short. We'd been straddled as it were and knew where the third shell would fall. We heard the approaching shriek and heard it fall right outside the shelter. I went outside. When the first shell had come the youngsters who'd called me windy had crawled into a culvert under the bank. The third shell had fallen immediately in front of it and they had all been killed by the blast.

We took part in the attack on Menin during mid-October 1918. It was a foggy morning and after heavy bombardment the air itself seemed somehow thick. The Germans replied with everything they had, including mustard gas. My friend, Corporal Wickens, and I were laying a telephone wire as we went forward into the thick fog. After we'd reached our immediate objective we had to retrace our steps many times in order to repair the line as it was smashed regularly by exploding shells. We had to do all this wearing gas masks with fog blurring the outside and condensation – because we were sweating – blurring the inside. At one stage in spite of the gas all around us we had to take them off to clear them so we could see. This wasn't nearly as dangerous as it sounds because if you kept the nose-clip pinching your nostrils and clamped your lips tightly round the mouthpiece without speaking it was really quite safe. Corporal Wickens won a well-deserved DCM as a result of that day's work.

It is very difficult to talk about bravery and cowardice in war because these are such complex things, or at least I think they are. I think that many cases of shell-shock were caused by the ordinary infantryman having to just sit there and take everything that came his way. A stretcher-bearer, for example, was better off – he could busy himself with the wounded and a signal linesman was always active mending lines broken by the shelling. Here a man might be brave because he was afraid but continued to carry out his obligations. And sometimes bravery and cowardice are affected by poor health, lack of sleep, physical wretchedness and so on. Many men who went to France came from such poverty-stricken backgrounds that they were underdeveloped and undernourished even before the test of war began. Many routine jobs might, with hindsight, seem brave simply because they were carried out under dangerous conditions. When we were holding out against the Germans on Mount Kemmel, for example, I was told by the signal officer to go out and find the signal office of the 11th Queens, which was somewhere on our left at the other side of the hill. There was no moon so it was pitch-black and having found the 11th Queens signal office I had to run a line across the face of the hill from that office to our own. I had never seen this hill in daylight and had to traverse its shell-pocked face by night with an occasional barrage of shells bursting on it and traversed by enemy machine-gun fire.

A friend has told me since that he was very glad I'd been picked for the job and that he had not rated my chances of getting through very highly. I didn't feel that way about it at all because I was being forced to do something, I was active. I ran out one reel of wire from the 11th Queens, but having no more wire I had to continue across the hill to our office to get more. I hoped to retrace my steps and find the loose end when I returned which is exactly what I did. This was a routine job – dangerous, but one had to do it. What takes real courage is going from a dug-out into a trench that you know is being shelled. What takes even more courage is to go from the trench up on to the top in full view of the enemy and stay there moving forward in spite of the fact that all around you men are being blown to pieces and cut apart by machine-gun fire.

One extraordinary episode which I will always remember occurred at Ypres in the summer of 1918. Days and dates at the time were meaningless so I don't know exactly when it was, June, July or August.

Anyway, I was at the transport lines at Brandhoek on the Ypres–Poperinge road. This was a time when both the Germans and the British seemed very suspicious of what was going on behind opposing lines on our sector. As a result each side had anything up to ten observation balloons in the air at any one time. Ours were in the air just west of Poperinge; the Germans had theirs in the Menin area, but we could see them quite plainly from where we were.

We were used to German planes coming over at night and machine-gunning our camps and horse lines, but it was unusual for them to come over during daylight at that stage of the war. Then, one day, a German plane did come over during the day with all eyes and anti-aircraft guns on it. We watched it as it flew towards us. It managed to avoid the anti-aircraft guns and made for the most northerly of our balloons which it fired on. Two figures jumped from the suspended baskets and two parachutes opened. The balloon on fire began to fall. The plane went from one balloon to the next until it had downed all our balloons in flames. From each basket two figures always jumped but some parachutes failed to open and others were set alight by burning fragments from the balloons and their speed of descent accelerated as the parachutes burned.

Thousands of soldiers watched this happening and we were furious but could do nothing. Then from the south came a British plane and as we watched the two planes bore down on each other. They swerved and fired and the German's engine seemed to stall. Then he bailed out and landed on the roof of a house at Poperinge. We cheered like mad things! But that wasn't the end of it because our airman then set off for the German line. He avoided the German anti-aircraft guns, flew to the most southerly balloon and next minute it was ablaze. He moved along from balloon to balloon till he'd destroyed them all and then returned unscathed to our lines. We cheered ourselves hoarse as we watched the scene unfold. To this day I do not know the airman's name nor if he was decorated for his bravery.

Food was a constant source of worry for front line soldiers. In Italy I remember we were always hungry, but we used to get *polenta* sometimes and fry it or use it like bread with jam. Once a friend and I used a coffee grinder to grind some wheat that we'd found and then we made chapattis out of it. In France the officers were always fed better than the troops, but we got porridge most days with a rasher of bacon on top of it and tea. When the going was good we would get a loaf of bread between five or six of us, but more often than not the day's ration of one loaf was shared between about twenty-five. Sometimes we had raisins instead of jam and the cooks would make a pudding of pulverized biscuits and raisins and water. The mixture had a gluey consistency. It would be wrapped roly-poly style in a sandbag and then boiled or steamed – delicious, apart from all the bits from the sandbag that got stuck to it and ended up being eaten! It didn't do to be too fussy.

Sandbags were constantly used to cook in and to carry food around in. Once cooked at the transport lines the food would be brought to the front line trenches under cover of darkness. Tea came up in petrol tins but it was usually pretty awful – I used to put cocoa cubes in mine to improve the taste but it didn't make a lot of difference.

Soldiers in my experience were always a little superstitious. We were a hard-headed lot and not given to worrying about walking under ladders or spilling salt (largely because we didn't have these things at the front!) but there were things of which we were mortally afraid. One was the Queen's Death Song. It was a very popular song in those days but in the battalion it was absolutely forbidden to be sung, hummed or whistled and if by chance it was sung by a visiting concert party we would all walk out. Too many deaths had followed the singing of that song. Men often had a premonition of death too. I remember one instance at Busseboom when we were in reserve. Headquarters signallers were in a sandbagged shelter at the rear of a farmhouse and our cooks were established in a nearby barn. Smoke from the cookers in the salient usually made the Germans start shelling the cooking areas and the tracks leading to those areas. Latrine tracks were given the same treatment. Across the other side of the road which ran in front of the farmhouse were B Company trenches and one evening, as I went for a stroll along the road, I saw in the distance a lone man staggering along carrying a full pack. As he came closer I saw it was a friend of mine, Jack Daley, the corporal in charge of B Company. He was returning from 14 days leave in Blighty. His face was a picture of despair so I tried to cheer him up. I chaffed him about returning from leave in such a state of mind. 'I shan't go back again Dick,' he said sadly. I tried again to take him out of his mood and told him he was only feeling bad because just a few hours earlier he'd been at home. 'No Dick,' he said 'I know I'm going to stop one.' Next morning when 'cookhouse' was sounded by the buglers Jack volunteered to get the company dixie from the cooker. He got out of his trench and walked a few paces along the track that led to the cookhouse and a shell blew him to pieces.

Sometimes men died because they couldn't stand the circumstances of a particular situation any longer. At Dickebusche in August 1918, for example, B Company had just made an abortive attack from behind a railway embankment. Driven back to the embankment they had to leave their wounded behind. The cries and groans of these wounded men proved too much for a chap called Lacchary Wood, an Irishman who wore the Mons Ribbon. 'I can't stand this any longer,' he said and got up from behind the bank to try to get one of the injured men in. He was shot through the head and died instantly.

The war had curious effects on people. Former Sunday school teachers would suddenly turn into terrific swearers and although I don't think there was as much womanizing – or going with prostitutes – as is sometimes imagined, the men did often indulge in excessive drinking. But who can blame them? And whatever excesses there were they were more than offset by the comradeship and humour found in the ranks. Peacetime had nothing to touch it.

That was why it was such a shock to me when I returned to civilian life. I managed to get a job with some stationers in Finsbury, North London, through a friend who knew my parents. One of the first things the general manager of this firm impressed on me was the fact that there was no sentiment in business – in other words no one was going to take war service into account now it was over. How right he was! Neither he nor the boss had served during the war but in the boardroom they had a massive picture of the ruined cloth hall at Ypres. The managing director was very proud of having taken the picture himself but I always felt that he wouldn't have hung around long enough to take that picture if he'd been there when I was there. The women and younger men had filled all the vacancies while we were away and of course they didn't want to give up their jobs when we returned. The troops had a mnemonic for that: FYJIA – meaning 'Fuck You Jack I'm Alright!'

My job with the stationers was temporary and when it ended I went on the dole along with about one million other men. We got 15s. a week and, of course, I applied for every job I thought I could do. I remember I applied for a job as a temporary clerk at the Ministry of Labour offices in Whitehall. At the place where the appointments were made I filled in a form stating my rank in the army, my education, army courses I'd attended and army exams I'd passed, length of service etc. I was then called before a board of bearded old men. The chairman, funnily enough, was a Mr Dixon and he was the only even remotely young man among them. I was told that my application form had been considered but that I had no experience. I was so angry that I stood up and said, 'Gentlemen, you are completely mistaken. I've had more experience than anyone in this room. When I joined the army in 1914 I told the recruiting sergeant that I couldn't ride a horse. He said, "We'll bloody teach you" and they did. And they spared no pains over it. Apparently I can be fitted for war but not for peace. I shall know what to do another time gentlemen. Good day.' And I walked out.

This was the climate when we got back, yet everyone had done their utmost before and during the war to remind us of our duty. Women and young girls even went around giving out white feathers, but that was all forgotten when we returned and you could tell that having fought for five years suddenly meant nothing. It was a shock, I can tell you. Even later on it was remarkable how people wanted to forget all about the war. At one interview for a job as a headmaster much later in my career, two female members of the board who were interviewing me, when told about my war service, said, 'We want to forget all about that.' I was indignant and said, 'If you can, certainly, but personally I cannot.' The elderly chairman of the board then said, 'You see, Mr Dixon, whenever a criminal is brought before the magistrates in London he always pleads that he is an ex-serviceman.' My reply was more polite than they deserved but I told them I was not a criminal and that I was not pleading. Then I left. The old men still had the last word, and although the returning men had new ideas, the old order still had a great hold on people.

During the war people could be very kind though. I remember on a home leave in August 1917 a marvellous incident. I'd suffered seasickness on the crowded troop ship but it was worth it as I watched the white cliffs of Dover draw ever nearer. And how my eyes feasted on the countryside as the train sped up through Kent. I looked forward to Victoria Station and the sights of London which I wanted to remember when I returned to France. Anyway, I walked out of Victoria Station carrying my rifle and my sword, a haversack, waterbottle, gas mask and tin hat. Anyone dressed like that was obviously either going to or coming from the front. As it was late afternoon it would have been assumed that I was going on leave.

Outside the station I waited with a huge crowd for a bus to take me to Waterloo where I could catch the train home to Woking. There was no queueing in those days – it really was unheard of – and there was just a mad scramble when the bus came. After the crowded troop ship and the trenches I couldn't bear what looked like another battle so I stayed right at the back of the skirmishing. Suddenly a brawny flower woman caught the handrail of the bus, pushed her basket into the faces of the foremost in the crowd and shouted, 'Come on, my boy. You've done your bit. Come on.' The crowd fell back and feeling a little proud and a little humble I said thank you to everyone and climbed up the stairs to get a better look at dear old London. All the buses in those days had their stairs on the outside and they were open topped. On another occasion I was given leave and arrived at Victoria Station. I was carrying a lot of gear and I'd just passed through the ticket barrier when a very elderly gentleman with a white beard simply leant towards me and said, 'God bless you, my boy.'

Leave was enjoyed in so many different ways by different soldiers. Some stayed in bed half the day, others took to wine, women and song. For myself I remember spending the day in London finishing up at Chu Chin Chow. The rest of the time I spent cycling through the unspoiled Surrey countryside which I loved, visiting friends and relatives of friends I'd left at the front. When you went on leave men always asked you to tell their relatives things that could not be put on the censored letters they were allowed to send from the trenches.

During the last days of my leave in 1918 I was standing at the gate of my home in Woking when a battalion of A4 infantry passed by. A4 infantry were basically new recruits. I was wearing civilian clothes and one of them shouted at me, 'When are you going to join up, mate?' I felt like punching him on the nose but instead said, '1914, old man.' His face was a picture and his immediate companions turned and jeered at him. An officer broke ranks and gave him a dressing down. Honour, I thought, was satisfied.

I've always been rather anti-establishment. I think the war did that for me, but there were also particular incidents. I remember the fuss that was made, for example, when we heard that the king was coming to view the troops at the front. We were holding the line east of Dickebusche in front of Scottish Wood and near Dead Dog Farm on 2 August 1918 when all the older soldiers (length of service, not age) were withdrawn to the transport line. We spent the next day polishing our boots and equipment and those with clothing unfit for parade were given new uniforms. I believe we were also given a shower. On 4 August we were marched to a light railway on which we travelled several miles to a village called Winnezeele. Here we got out of the roofless trucks and marched into the main street of the village. It had begun to rain. Then we received a very peculiar order – to fall out and look as if we were at rest. Further down the street were contingents from other regiments. What we all had in common was the Mons Star or 1915 medal ribbons; many were NCOs; all had one red chevron and some blue chevrons. We were then ordered to stand at ease and look natural! Then the explanation came. King George V was to pass that way any minute. We were also ordered to cheer at a given signal. By this time it was raining heavily. Then the king arrived and spasmodic cheering broke out, but it was neither loud nor continuous, probably because the troops realized they were being used to put on a show for the king and they resented it. Our captain – Captain Girling – said he was not pleased with our response to his order and hoped we would respond with more enthusiasm when the king returned. Needless to say the return journey was treated in the same way. We then went back to the transport lines and those given new uniforms had to get back into their rags. When the king passed he looked very depressed!

As a signaller I should say something about the different methods we used to communicate. We used the D3 field telephone for verbal and coded messages, but the system was vulnerable to German equipment that picked up messages by induction from the land lines. Instead we used what was called the Fullerphone, which had a constant buzz that the Germans could hear and on which was superimposed morse signals that the Germans could not hear. Then there was the telephone exchange 4+3 used at HQ to receive land lines from the companies. We also had something called a power buzzer and amplifier, a ground wireless system that was easily monitored and was therefore only useful for SOS purposes to the artillery. We had the Lucas lamp with different coloured light filters – it was carried in a box and used on a tripod.

Other methods included the message rocket which produced a high-pitched scream as it flew through the air. The noise was designed to help you locate it when it came down. There was a thing called the Popham Panel, a blue sheet of cloth 12 ft wide with flaps that could be opened to reveal white patterns to signal to aeroplanes. Flags were also used, together with despatch riders on motorbikes, and, of course, there were also horses and pigeons. The latter were highly reliable but tended to be fired at by the enemy. Dogs were also used and they could be very good, but they were spoiled by contact with the front line troops who fed them. At one time this got so bad that orders were issued making it an offence to feed a message dog.

In front of the ramparts at Ypres in 1918 we had an exceptionally good dog that used to reach our brigade HQ in just twenty minutes. Verey Lights – a kind of flare – were also used, and runners – that is human runners. Men were used when land lines had been destroyed by shell fire, but this was a very dangerous undertaking if you were unlucky enough to be picked for it.

When my career got going I trained as a teacher and eventually became headmaster of Ripley Church School in Surrey. I stayed there from 1936 till 1961 when I retired. The school was pulled down years ago, but I have happy memories of that time and believe I did some good in changing some of the old, foolish ways in which lessons were taught.

CHAPTER FOUR

FREDERICK JAMES HODGES

'He was running at me through the mist. A very young man, fit, as we all were, but he was running too fast. It was unnatural. Then, as he came towards me, I noticed that the right side of his steel helmet was missing together with part of the right side of his head. His mouth was open and his face covered in blood. He ran towards me through the mist and then vanished. I never saw him again.' Though he is now ninety-three Frederick James Hodges still remembers with absolute clarity that vision from the inferno. For him the Great War started in the trenches, but ended with the big breakthrough of 1918 and, after fierce fighting, the defeat of the Germans on the ground and in and around the rubble of the villages of France and Belgium.

I was at Northampton Grammar School when war broke out and it wasn't until March 1918 that there was any chance of my seeing action. March 1918 is significant because it was the month when the Germans broke through our lines. We'd lost so many young men that the British government decided it was time to reduce the call up age from eighteen years and nine months to eighteen, with the proviso that the men should not be sent on active service until they reached nineteen. The problem was that Russia had thrown in the towel and the Germans therefore had no problem with a second front. They could hurl all their forces at the Western Front. Some 5,000 big guns and almost a million men were moved from the Eastern to the Western Front. And with this overwhelming strength the Germans were able to break through. The British Army had grown smaller and smaller as thousands of young men were killed. There were no more eighteen- and nineteen-year-olds to call up so we seventeen-year-old boys received our call up. I joined up with a couple of chums and was sent to Tollgate Camp near Harwich.

The German offensive that started in March didn't get very far. They got bogged down after a month or two of movement and with each attempt to get around the trenches, rather than across them, the length of the front increased. We ended up with a 400 mile front. The northern part was British, the southern French.

The British had treated their section like home for years and battalions had time after time taken over each other's trenches. But when we arrived in 1918 we were sent through to a non-existent front. The Germans had blurred all the frontiers. And after their big offensive we didn't start fighting back until August when ANZAC burst through. My battalion – I was a corporal – was backing them up and soon after the start I was made battalion gas NCO.

Even at eighteen – I'd just reached that age when I arrived in France – it is surprising what you could get used to. You had to react to circumstances and you did.

One of my strongest memories is of reaching Thiepval Ridge where we lost more than 50,000 men in 1916. The area was still totally devastated when we reached it and all through the autumn of 1918 we attacked time and again, but at least we were out of the trenches, moving forward. By November resistance had collapsed because the Americans had arrived and the Germans didn't stand a chance.

The Americans brought their planes and we had tanks by then. These early tanks were heavy steel and iron and very clumsy with a curious rounded shape. I remember that they used to run out of petrol very quickly. For seven months we lived in a kind of mist, moving forward and stopping only to sleep. Only those who were hit stopped moving. And you could be hit at any time – there were bullets everywhere. You felt them as they flew through the air.

Every night while we were still in the trenches a party of men would make the long dangerous trek to a sunken road or to the back of a wood, where the company quartermaster-sergeant and his men dished out the rations. Our rations were brought up from the horse lines, usually situated in a wood or a deserted railway station. The quartermaster-sergeant's area was a mess of wagons, horses, mules, tents and stores, to which the Army Service Corps brought supplies from their depots even further back behind the front. Sometimes enemy shell fire would penetrate this far back and there would be casualties among the men, the horses and the mules. The sickly-sweet smell of dead mules would drift to our trenches until someone could find time to bury them.

When the rations had all been dished out, the ration party, loaded with sandbags full of loaves, cheese, jam, tobacco, cigarettes, matches and tins of bully beef, made the long trek back to Company HQ. Here the rations were divided between four platoons, and then between the four sections in each platoon.

I was made to establish a post near Martinbush. We were in a long, narrow, grassy gully and we were continually showered with howitzers. I can still remember the stinging smell of the cordite. Within five minutes of setting up our post two of my companions had been shot dead and two more were wounded.

We were always studying maps because everywhere we went looked the same – grey, smashed and unchanging, but we had to try to find out what was in front of us. And it was only after a few weeks of fighting that I realized how little training we'd been given.

We'd been taught to march, to stand upright and to fire our guns, but that was about it. I'd been put in the 53rd Young Soldiers' Battalion Lancashire Fusiliers and every boy in that battalion was the same age to within a fortnight. We had enlisted at seventeen and were considered fit for duty as soon as we were eighteen. The German push came on 21 March 1918 and on 24 March we were told we were being sent to the front. So off I went with my friends from Northampton Grammar School.

From my early weeks in France I now have only a haphazard series of memories. I remember being sent, for example, through a gas chamber to test my mask and then time seems to concertina and my next memory is of being in no man's land cutting barbed wire and keeping absolutely stock-still as a lurid green flare sailed up above us from the German trenches.

It was decided after a few months that I should be sent on a two-week gas course, to learn how to deal with mustard and other gas attacks and to teach the other men in my platoon when I returned. I learned everything I could, but when I got back there was no platoon to teach. They'd all been killed. I was told that Jerry had made a vicious trench raid during my absence, and by questioning a number of different soldiers I gradually found out what had happened.

The German gunners had put down a very heavy box barrage, which had completely isolated the section of trench occupied by No. 2 Platoon, preventing any reinforcement. It was all over in a few minutes. Picked German troops had entered our front line, probably through the old 1916 trenches which I had helped to block with barbed wire. Everyone in my old platoon had been killed, wounded or taken prisoner. Those down in the sap (a covered trench) were trapped and either killed or severely wounded. The German troops had evidently known about the sap and threw down some of our own Mills bombs which were conveniently stacked in wooden boxes nearby. Among those taken prisoner were the officer on duty, Corporal Croot, the young soldier who took charge of us on our journey from Calais to the battalion, Lance-Corporal Singleton, my section leader, and about a dozen others whom I knew well. Sergeant Mercer, my platoon sergeant, had both legs shattered by a Mills bomb, and many others had been badly wounded.

My firsthand account eventually came when a young chap called Wenderleish, with whom I'd been ever since we came to France, returned from hospital some weeks later. He had been wounded in the upper arm, a flesh wound, during the preliminary shelling, which he described as terrific. He saw the German troops, all big chaps, leap into our front line and, while some used our Mills bombs, others grabbed the officer, Corporal Croot, Lance-Corporal Singleton and others. He said they lifted them up out of the trench to other German troops who hustled them across no man's land to the German front line.

Wenderleish saw all this happen, fascinated by the precision and the speed of the raid. 'All over in no time,' he said. Then, clutching his wound with his other hand to try to stop the bleeding, he bolted down the communication trench and reached the battalion first-aid post.

Many years later, I read the official account of this incident, which occurred on 4 June 1918.

At 2.30 a.m. the Germans commenced a furious bombardment with guns and trench mortars against the front held by the 10th Battalion of the Lancashire Fusiliers. At 2.40 a.m., they lifted the barrage to the support line and continued to bombard it and the flanks, thus creating a box barrage.

As the barrage lifted from the front line to the support line, parties of well-armed Germans, who had used the old trenches crossing the new no man's land, broke into the battalion's trenches on a frontage of several hundred yards, overcoming the garrison on the left flank. On the right they were met by vigorous Lewis gun fire, and Lance-Corporal H.J. Colley with two men bombed along the trench and succeeded in ejecting the intruders.

Many casualties were inflicted on the Germans, but the Lancashire Fusiliers lost one officer and twelve other ranks killed, twenty-one men wounded and two officers and thirteen other ranks taken prisoner. Lance-Corporal Colley was awarded the Military Medal for clearing the trench with Mills bombs.

I spent only a few weeks in the trenches before we moved forward day after day, travelling in mist and smoke over ground smashed and gouged up into a state of indescribable desolation. I was involved in attack after attack, but by sheer luck I was never even scratched. The town of Neuville took a week to capture, for example, and we lost 180 men, but I seemed to lead a charmed life. And we were all so fit. We were at the top of our physical form – we had to be. Anything less and you were quickly finished.

The gas we had to put up with was always terrible. In many ways it was harder to cope with than the shelling and sniper fire. To die by gas was terrible, particularly the phosgene which mixed with your blood and created a deathly compound. It smelled of pineapple, such an innocent smell but a killer. One of my jobs was to post gas sentries and the sentry would swing a football rattle round and round or beat a big cartridge case if he sensed gas approaching. But the whole gas thing was more complicated than many people now think. The Germans would send over a gas that would only make you sneeze and the men wouldn't bother to put on their masks. Then they'd send over the deadly stuff, hoping we'd be caught napping and be killed.

I remember Mormal Forest which took us three days to get through. Wilfred Owen was killed here. French women and children would occasionally greet us as we travelled forward. '*Vive les Anglais*' they would shout.

But the war was to end suddenly for me. A despatch rider simply rode up to us out of the blue and said the Germans had all gone. I was back in England by February 1919 having marched 60 miles to Abbeville from the front. We travelled on an old river steamer to Southampton and everywhere there were stalls offering us fruit and sandwiches. It was so marvellous to be on a real train after those awful French cattle trucks.

I went to Purfleet to be demobilized and received my official discharge that summer together with £12 in pay. None of my clothes fitted any more when I got back to Northampton, where I was to spend the next forty-five years working for the gas board. I'd had enough excitement for one lifetime!

Mailly-Maillet is a village I knew only in darkness until I revisited it in 1965. During the weeks I spent in the trenches at Auchonvillers – this was during my first couple of months in France – we often passed through Mailly-Maillet as we took part in various working parties and ration parties. All the houses in the village were badly damaged by shell fire and it was an eerie place where enemy shells burst continually in the street as we ran through at dead of night. A long high wall ran down one side of the main street and behind this lay a chateau. Both the wall and the chateau were badly damaged, the gardens and statues and greenhouses smashed and broken.

I suppose my strongest memories of my months at the front – and for most of us that experience was life changing after the quiet of our Edwardian childhoods – are of the very precise period 8 August 1918 to 11 November 1918. During those weeks we were always on the move. I'm certain we never spent two nights in the same place. The faces of our officers changed continually as they were killed or injured – the casualty rate among the junior officers was terrific.

At a place called Talmas my platoon officer gave me a box of rifle grenades, some special blank cartridges and a metal cup to attach to my rifle in place of my bayonet. This cup held a rifle grenade, basically a Mills bomb with a short metal rod screwed into its base. I disliked being the platoon's rifle grenadier, because the blank cartridge made the rifle barrel filthy, which would get me in trouble with my platoon officer when he made his twice daily inspection. A few weeks later, I joined another platoon and quietly went back to being a rifleman.

I'd never used a rifle grenade, but it was very useful for collecting flowers – I used to put poppies from the fields in the metal cup on the rifle. Most of the men thought nothing of flowers, but I was always aware of them growing in the midst of so much destruction. There were poppies everywhere and a few other wild flowers, but they made that period of May, June and July 1918 unforgettably poignant. Between the devastated villages, the crops lay ungathered and I have never before or since been so acutely aware of life.

This was enhanced by the humour of those days and I remember that well. It wasn't all horror and gloom. It was more short bursts of tremendous activity when dozens would be killed and injured followed by long, sometimes boring bouts of inactivity. When we joined up and got our uniforms I remember Tim Costello and another friend and I went to Woolworths and bought red, white and blue ribbon which we tied on our hats. Then, to commemorate the occasion, we had our photograph taken in a studio with the three of us proudly wearing our ribbons.

I suppose I was in quite a small group of soldiers who experienced trench warfare *and* the final breakthrough that led to hand to hand fighting in the villages and towns. In Neuville I remember we chased the Germans through ruined houses. One of my friends died as a result of a very brave action here. He broke into the back of a house, killed two Germans and then rushed out into the street to try to surprise a sniper who'd kept us pinned down for hours. He got the sniper but was fatally wounded himself. He was awarded the VC. Sometimes officer after officer would be killed trying to knock out a sniper or a well entrenched machine-gun post.

I remember on one occasion we had to move up an area of sloping ground. As we went forward we spotted some Germans so we took cover to wait for our machine-gunners to come up behind. When the time came to move again one of our young officers simply got up and went forward. He was shot dead seconds later. Another young officer took his place and he too was killed.

During my first weeks at the front I just couldn't believe how casually death and injury were treated. But large numbers of casualties were inevitable with millions of men engaged in pitched battles, trench raids and general shelling. In the great battles at Loos, Neuve Chapelle, Arras, Ypres and the Somme, hundreds of thousands of men were killed or wounded. A battalion occupying what everyone thought of as a quiet sector usually lost about twenty men in a tour of duty.

When we relieved another battalion we always asked, 'Have you had many casualties?' The answer might well be, 'No, about a dozen. It's very quiet here – but watch out for snipers.' Along the immense length of the Western Front the casualties added up to thousands of course. Routine deaths were usually the result of sniper bullets, shrapnel and chance shells. Such deaths were a terrible waste, but they were unavoidable given that we had to hold the line. While we held the line men were going to die!

But the war we experienced in 1918 was very different from the war of 1914–17 because in those first years each side desperately tried to get round the other by extending the front line further and further and all to no avail.

After this great length of time, the Great War must seem almost like a medieval war to some people – everything drawn by horses and wagons, everywhere floundering in mud.

I suppose it was medieval in some ways but there was no resentment between the men and the officers. Ordinary soldiers like me thought a lot of our officers, particularly the junior officers. On the other hand, I think we were extremely critical of the generals. They never came near the front and we knew they were living in relative comfort. There was also virtually no risk of them being injured or killed.

It took a long time for the army to realize that the supply of young men was limited and, in an effort to cut down casualties, the front line was eventually much more thinly manned. About 100 yards behind the front line was what was known as the close support trench from which a counter-attack could be made.

Clarrie Jarman (right) and two friends, photographed a few days before the first Battle of the Somme. Though badly injured, Clarrie is the only one of the three to have survived

Clarrie Jarman

No. 6 Platoon, B Company, 7th Battalion, The Queen's, during training at Purfleet Camp, 1914. Clarrie is standing fifth from the right

A studio portrait of Richard Hawkins, probably taken in 1915

The Lochnager Crater. Two minutes before the Battle of the Somme began, the huge Lochnager Mine was exploded beneath a German strongpoint close to the village of La Boisselle. The vast crater, over 300 ft wide and almost 90 ft deep, remains to this day

Fred Dixon's platoon photographed during their last weeks in England. Fred is seated, front row, third from the left

A hastily-dug grave on the Somme

Members of C Squadron, Surrey (Q.M.R.) Yeomanry moving forward in March 1917.
In spite of the dominance of the machine-gun thousands of cavalry horses were kept ready
in reserve. (Photograph courtesy of the Imperial War Museum)

Fred Dixon in 1916, a studio portrait

A silhouette of Fred's profile cut in Cologne in 1919

Fred, aged 20, in regulation issue winter sheepskin in Ailly-sur-Somme during the winter of 1916/17 – remembered as 'one of the severest in modern human experience'

A formal portrait of Fred Dixon and his comrade from the Surrey Yeomanry, Jimmy Hole.

Fred and a group of friends photographed while training with the Surrey Yeomanry in Dorking in 1914. Fred is seated in the centre

Fred Hodges, (standing, left) with three friends soon after joining up

Fred and a friend are carefully indicated on a photograph taken while on parade at Tollgate Camp, summer 1917

Fred Hodges

Further back was the reserve line with Company HQ, and still further back Battalion HQ.

The front line soldier never had an overall perspective of the battle. He only ever knew that if he was in the front line when the Germans attacked, he and all his comrades were expendable and might be sacrificed for some distant strategic decision made by a general miles behind the front line.

I was one of the soldiers who discovered firsthand just how scientific had been the German preparations for a long war. This came about when we were told to move into a German sap. I didn't know what a sap was at the time, but I soon found out. The one we were to occupy had obviously been there for quite some time. It had been dug into the side of the trench and deep down into the pure chalk. Since the enemy had dug it, it was facing the wrong way for us with the two openings in what, from our point of view, was the rear wall of the trench. Each opening was about 4 ft high and 3 ft wide and led down a shaft at about forty-five degrees, with steps cut into the slope, which led to a big, dark chamber about 25 ft below.

This chamber measured about 20 ft by 7 or 8 ft. Its walls and ceiling glistened with moisture in the candle-light, which was the only light we had apart from the daylight which filtered down the two shafts. The sap gave us protection from enemy shell fire, but I found it cold, damp and very uncomfortable. I could never sleep in it when it was my turn to lie down for a few hours, and I also had an uneasy feeling that one could easily be trapped there.

While we were in the sap Company HQ was in a cellar that had been half blown in and then strengthened and propped up with sandbags. Not very far away was our front line, which was in a very dangerous position because it could be fired at directly from higher ground in enemy hands.

Anyway, once our sentries had been posted and the Lewis gun positions manned, those of us who were free for the time being began to explore our territory, make improvements where possible and explore the trench system, such as it was, to get the feel of our own section and its relation to our flanks.

Late at night on 11 July about thirty of us were led by Lieutenant Drummond, second-in-command of A Company, to a position beyond our own rather ragged front line. We scrambled out of the trench and followed him quietly in a half left direction. Eventually we came to a partly dug trench in no man's land which had evidently been started by previous working parties. The trench varied in depth from 3 to 6 ft, and as soon as we got there Lieutenant Drummond told us to start digging with as little noise as possible. I was working in a shallow part with two older men named Carpenter and Fisher – as luck would have it both my companions were miners who made my efforts look puny by comparison.

We were quite close to the outskirts of the town of Albert, which was in German hands, and their flares probably gave our position away. We'd made little progress with our digging when suddenly we came under fierce shell fire. I crouched in the shallow trench, holding my spade close to my face for protection from shell splinters. We joked about the lucky ones who had spades and the unlucky ones who had only a pickaxe for protection, but we could do nothing except stick it out until the shelling ceased. When that eventually happened and things got a little quieter we were told by our sergeant to move along to a deeper part of the trench for greater safety. We had to step over two or three of our dead lying in the bottom of the deeper part of the trench and a little further on we found some wounded, including Lieutenant Drummond, who was standing on the top, looking down into the trench and calmly directing those wounded men who could walk. He helped several to climb out and sent them back to our front line. Very little was accomplished by the working party, but while a stretcher-bearer bandaged Drummond's bleeding wrist, he stood and joked with us and then led us back to our own line. We never saw him again after that night, and many of us greatly missed him. He had a great gift for leadership, inspiring us by his courage and by his genuine personal interest in us. This was especially true when it came to boys newly arrived at the front.

I still remember the time we first experienced intense shell fire. Lieutenant Drummond told us to crouch on the fire-step – the raised platform at the front of the trench – with our backs to the trench wall, drawing up our knees to our chins and covering our faces with our arms. 'Now,' he said, 'you have covered your vital parts and there is nothing else to be done but to stick it out until Jerry stops shelling, and', he said, 'if any of you do stop one, well, what better way to die than in the front line for your King and Country.' That was a spirit which appealed very strongly to the men of eighteen in those critical days in the spring of 1918. We were fortunate in having such good officers; Lieutenant Drummond, the second-in-command of A Company and 2nd Lieutenant Stott, my first platoon officer, were two of the best of the many officers I served under on the Western Front.

The spirit of those far-off days may now seem rather quaint. Two world wars have receded into the past. New generations have been born who know nothing of war. Remembrance Sunday touches few chords of personal experience, except among the dwindling number of people who can remember those times. In its earlier form, as Armistice Day, the whole population shared haunting memories and emotions in a nationwide two minute silence, in which we renewed communication with our past and paid tribute to our dead.

On 13 July my platoon was moved into a section of the front line where immediately in front of our parapet the ground fell away quite steeply, so that one had the feeling of being in a grandstand overlooking no man's land. It was a very unusual situation. During daylight we could not move many yards to our right because the trench petered out to a depth of only about 18 in.

During the night the two sentries on duty kept in contact with the company on our right about 100 yards away. We did this by a regular patrol. One of us would go quietly along the shallow trench, feeling very exposed, especially when the German flares went up. Then about twenty minutes later one of the sentries from the other company would pay us a visit. We also visited one another when we were without a light for a cigarette.

One day I crawled out of the back of our trench and explored an old unused trench in which there were several dug-outs, blown in during fighting two years earlier. There were many interesting relics of that period, and I discovered that it led diagonally from our short, rather isolated stretch of front line, to another old 1916 trench from which our own Stokes trench mortars fired over our heads at the German positions.

We had been warned by the troops we relieved to watch out for a German sniper who, they said, sometimes occupied a little ditch near a tree stump out in no man's land. There was little we could do except keep our heads down, since to try to see him would be to become his target. One day our own boys tried firing Stokes mortars over our heads in an attempt to deal with him once and for all. We had mixed feelings about their efforts when pieces of red hot shrapnel came whirring back to us, threatening to decapitate the sentries. The British Stokes mortar was a simple weapon. It consisted of a metal base plate and a 3 in tube about 4 ft in length. The mortar had a 12-bore cartridge in its base which was detonated by a pin in the bottom of the tube when the 20 lb bomb was dropped into it.

The Stokes mortar was highly mobile, and a team could quickly set it up and fire fifty or even a hundred in a few minutes, with three or four in the air at once. The range was 200 to 500 yards. Naturally, this usually attracted some retaliation from the Germans, either in the form of shell fire or their trench mortars. Their big mortar, the *Minnenwerfer*, was a terrifying weapon; it fired a bomb up to 4 ft long, weighing 150 lb.

This enormous bomb had a deadly blast. I remember three boys – Fox, Willard and Waite – were killed by one during our first night in the trenches near Mesnil. The crater left by a *Minnenwerfer* was enormous, as big as a house, we used to say. Everyone felt absolutely helpless if we saw one coming. At night, the glowing fuse could be seen moving across the dark sky, and in daylight it was a small black dot in the sky growing bigger by the second as it came towards us. A high explosive shell has a trajectory and can be heard coming, but a Minnie just sails through the air, turning over and over with a 'swish-swish-swish' and then coming down almost vertically.

At Auchonvillers the Germans plastered us with shells. When this happened some men always decided to move to a certain part of the trench, perhaps a bit to the left or right because, for reasons best known to themselves, they thought they would be safer there; others remained where they were. It didn't really make a lot of difference and most of us were fatalistic about the whole thing. We used to say that if your number is on it, you'll get it wherever you are. In a funny way this could be a comforting attitude during a period of shelling, which occurred with teutonic regularity at Auchonvillers. We knew it would continue until the prescribed number of salvos had been fired, but sometimes one of our humorists would say, 'Now then, Jerry, that will do! You'll only hurt someone if you keep on.'

When, after about twenty minutes, the regular evening bombardment stopped, we would walk along the trench to see what damage had been done and find out if anyone had been hit. Gunga Dean (his name was Dean so we nicknamed him 'Gunga' because he was also our sanitary man) would check the latrine which was just behind the trench, and you could always hear him grumble if it had been damaged. You never got much sleep while in a trench, because you were either on sentry duty on the fire-step or working on trench repairs. At night some of us were sent back about a quarter of a mile through winding trenches to a sunken lane, where the horse transports unloaded fresh supplies of trench mortars. Others would fetch rations from the sunken lane and also carry up sandbags, reels of barbed wire, screw pickets, and boxes of Mills bombs.

There was always something to be done. One evening we suffered a direct hit from a German 5.9 in shell and three dead had to be buried and some wounded who could not walk had to be carried by stretcher, which was a difficult job for the stretcher-bearers in narrow winding trenches. Any spare time could always be filled with the never-ending work of repairing and strengthening our parapets with sandbags filled with soil from the back of the trench, but while you were doing this you had to keep a wary eye open for snipers.

If life in the trenches was dangerous – and it was certainly that – it was never dull. Something interesting was always happening I remember one beautiful summer evening looking back toward a string of British captive balloons. They were tethered behind a wood and hung lazily and motionless in a row. Then out of the blue – and this had been an unusually quiet evening – there was machine-gun fire, and a German plane began attacking the balloons. As we watched we saw the crews, two men from each basket, jump out and fall. We saw their parachutes open while the balloons burned and crumpled slowly to the ground. When the German pilot had set fire to the last of the balloons with incendiary bullets, he turned and swooped and fired at the men descending by their parachutes. Then diving to within a few feet of the ground, he came roaring towards us, actually passing right over me.

We all fired our rifles – every man within range had a go – but apparently we did no damage to him and he actually had the nerve to fire his machine-gun at us as he roared over. There were black crosses on the wings of the plane and I could see the pilot's goggled face as he streaked across no man's land and disappeared from sight.

Our rations were adequate – when they reached us. There was bread, cheese, jam, margarine, tea, bully beef in tins and sometimes Machonichies, a meat and vegetable ration we called M and V. Water, which was carried up in 2 gallon petrol cans, was usually flavoured with petrol and sometimes also with chloride of lime, presumably when the source of supply was suspect. The bread ration varied, four or five men to a loaf when we had recently received a new draft to replace casualties, or three to a loaf when we had recently suffered casualties but still received their rations. As the ration party came in sight, we always asked, 'How many to a bun?' and 'What are the cigs? Any Woodies?' Woodbines were always prized above other brands. White Cloud and other brands were hated because their green tobacco had a revolting, acrid taste and we suspected they'd been foisted on the government by fat profiteers who, we believed, smoked cigars themselves.

The issue of a tin of Fray Bentos bully beef was always greeted with great delight because it was the best brand, and also because bully beef was usually put directly into a stew with dried vegetables. I had never seen them before and wondered what was in two heavy sandbags I carried up one night slung across my shoulder. They were full of small, hard multi-coloured pieces that swelled into vegetables when soaked.

When it came to tea we liked it strong with condensed milk. Sometimes we had porridge, always known as *berghu*, which was one of the Indian names we'd picked up from the old soldiers who'd served in India in the days when, as they were always telling us, soldiering *was* soldiering! We used a number of other Indian words like *pozzi* for jam, *rooti* for bread, *char* for tea and *bundook* for rifle. If the company cook got a good fire going in a sheltered spot, perhaps in an abandoned building, he might even, on occasion, produce a roast and vegetables, and very occasionally we had fried bacon.

We cleaned our knives and forks by pushing them in and out of the earth, and wiping them on our puttees. The job of sanitary man, an important one, was usually given to an older, more experienced man who would dig a latrine behind the trench, usually enlarging or deepening a shell hole.

We had no water to wash with – none whatsoever! Sometimes we saved a little of our tea to shave in, and there was often water in nearby shell holes, but with this there was a risk of mustard gas contamination. And if you got mustard gas on your hands it caused deep, painful blisters. An old schoolfriend of mine, not in my battalion, was in hospital for months after washing his hands in a contaminated shell hole, and he bore the scars on the back of his hands for the rest of his life.

When very thirsty I sometimes drank from a clean puddle of rainwater. Proper drinking water in the trenches was always in very short supply and sometimes we were very thirsty indeed. If we were in a reserve trench we could sometimes get water from a village well. On one occasion I drank the water from a dead man's water-bottle. We were, however, strictly forbidden to drink the water in our own water-bottle. This was regarded as part of our iron rations, which included a tin of bully beef and some army biscuits. Our iron rations could be used only with the permission of an officer.

Once as I sat day dreaming, a shell burst with a loud crash just beyond the graves on the other side of the field track. A friend of mine, a chap called Widdowson, who had been in France for over three years, was quite unconcerned. He had survived several wounds and many battles, including Ypres and Passchendaele. He regarded a tour on the Somme battlefront as greatly preferable, despite its grim record.

By this stage of the war the small number of men in the battalion who had fought in some of the great battles of 1915, 1916 and 1917 spoke of those days as history. 'When we were in the old front line,' they would say, meaning before the big Somme offensive of 1916.

For us, the young soldiers of 1918, the task was to finish the war. The thinly held line of General Gough's 5th Army was now heavily reinforced. We had resisted the German 1918 spring offensive and the tide was about to turn.

But while we waited for this to happen we had to survive the shells and the snipers. A turning point came on 5 August 1918 when I was detailed for an advance party, consisting of one officer and five

NCOs, one from each of the four companies, A, B, C and D, and myself from the Battalion HQ Company. When we had all assembled and the officer had been briefed by the adjutant, the little party of six set off, marching along various field tracks behind the front.

We marched about 25 miles south, from Forceville to Fouilly near Villers-Bretonneux. We did not know where we were going, or why. Actually we were on our way to take part in the Battle of Amiens, which was to be the turning point in the war.

We slogged along in the summer heat and as we marched, men in dug-outs and bivouacs along our route looked at us with great curiosity. They wanted to know where this urgent little party was off to. Anything out of the ordinary always attracted attention, and rumours quickly grew and spread. But we could tell them nothing; no one knew anything yet about the coming British offensive. Our sense that something big was about to happen grew because there was evidence of strict security. When we came to Heilly there was an expeditionary force canteen with a crowd of men round it. We tried to approach but we were stopped by military police and prevented even from speaking to the New Zealanders crowding round it. This was the first time I had seen the New Zealand men. I was surprised that some were black, and I learned they were Maoris. The ANZACS (Australian and New Zealand Army Corps) had been secretly moved south ready for what was to prove an historic attack on 8 August and we were being moved south to mop up.

Mopping up was necessary to prevent the enemy emerging from dug-outs behind advancing troops and attacking them from the rear. There was also a need to ensure that enemy wounded were disarmed, cases having occurred when they too fired on troops who had passed by them. There was one tough and very experienced officer of whom it was said that he never left any wounded enemy soldiers behind him.

By this stage of the war the infantry had been relieved of their heavy packs, and had adopted fighting order or battledress. This consisted of belt and braces, haversack on the back in place of the valise or pack, rolled groundsheet, entrenching tool, water-bottle, gas mask worn on the chest in the alert position, steel helmet, rifle and bayonet, 120 rounds of ammunition, Mills bomb in each breast pocket, and more in a spare haversack if desired.

The haversack held a mess tin, towel and shaving kit, extra socks, iron rations (tin of bully beef and army biscuits) and any personal items. Stretcher-bearers carried a rolled stretcher in lieu of a rifle and wore an armlet marked SB. Signallers carried heavy signalling equipment, reels of telephone wire, buzzers, carrier pigeons in a basket and aircraft signals (strips of coloured cloth which could be laid out on the ground for various purposes). Lewis gun teams carried their gun and many heavy panniers full of ammunition.

During the night of 19/20 August 1918 we arrived at the rear of the battle area. It was obvious that the big British offensive had begun here too. The Battalion HQ staff were drastically thinned out; various trades such as the tailors, the boot repairers and clerks being kept in the rear with the transport at Acheux.

With the rest of our troops, we moved forward from Acheux over familiar field tracks, with the well-known village of Mailly-Maillet on our left, and Englebelmer on our right, we came to our old reserve line and found it empty. We thought it very strange to go on from there to our old front line trenches in daylight, and to find them empty too. In the past we had always scuttled through Mailly-Maillet or Mesnil in the dark and often under enemy fire. Then another strange thing happened. Our rations were brought up to us instead of us having to go back from the trenches to fetch them. To our further amazement, they included a large juicy joint of raw meat! A joint of meat was very unusual at any time, and in the present state of affairs very inappropriate because we were going into action, and there would be no opportunity for the company cook to do anything with it.

During 20 August we passed beyond our old front line between Mesnil and Hamel, going downhill to the River Ancre and wading through lagoons of water, reeds and rushes. We came under fire here from behind – bullets whipped and whined past us. I'm sure they were fired by our supporting troops, who mistook us for retreating Germans. Corporal Wilkinson ordered one of our signallers to use his signalling lamp and flash a message back. This was quickly done and then the firing ceased.

Soon we came to a small stone bridge and some army pontoons over the river. Here we crossed to the old German front line which was deserted. At Ovillers we took our first prisoner. He was small, bearded and very docile. We found him lurking in a dug-out, one of a long row dug into an earth bank. Several of my old schoolfriends had been killed in this area and in our advance we crossed old grass-covered trenches that had been blown in and smashed by the 1916 shell fire. We saw the rotting remains of old sandbagged parapets, belts of machine-gun ammunition, rusty bayonets, cartridge clips and, among the flourishing weeds, graves.

On our right was Delville Wood, once an area of 150 acres of oak and birch, with dense hazel thickets, now blackened and shattered tree stumps. In 1916 the South African Infantry Brigade was ordered to take it at all costs. Of the 121 officers and 3,032 men who went into the attack on 14 July, only three officers and 140 men came out alive when they were relieved on 20 July.

As we continued our assault of Ovillers Ridge, away on our left was the site of the village of Thiepval. Before the war it was surrounded by apple orchards, and there were great trees in the beautiful park surrounding a lovely chateau. All we could see of where the chateau once stood was a mound of brick rubble.

Soon after this we moved again at dawn. We advanced through thick mist, whole battalions in line. At this stage there was no firing or shelling and it almost seemed as though we were simply on manœuvres. It was so strange – the silence and the long lines of men, only their heads and shoulders visible above the thick, white ground mist. Then the eerie silence was broken; ahead of us in the mist a German machine-gun began to fire. An officer of another company loomed up close to me in the thick mist and said 'Do you think he's just firing into the blue?' I said I thought he was but that we would be in trouble soon because the mist was lifting and it wouldn't be long before we were visible.

More machine-guns began to fire ahead of us, and although we suffered casualties no one near me was hit. We wondered why there was no enemy shell fire, and concluded that Jerry was withdrawing his guns. Our guns were silent too, as they were moving up to new positions.

At this stage of the battle everything was uncannily quiet. Then, as the mist began to clear, we came to the main road from Albert to Bapaume. I crossed it at an angle, leading about a dozen men, mostly regimental police, going down a steep bank on to the road. Machine-gun fire from the left came in fierce bursts as we ran across the road and dived into a big empty gun-pit that had been dug into a bank.

Wounded men who could walk were coming back down the road; some had head wounds, some were bleeding from an arm or shoulder. One man hobbled into the gun-pit with a large bloody field dressing on his leg above the knee; his trousers had been slit open and were flapping round his leg. Eventually we scrambled up and out of the gun-pit and joined other Lancashire Fusiliers who were moving towards Martinpuich. As we advanced up the long grassy slope, the German guns suddenly opened up on us again and shells began to burst just ahead of us.

There were no officers around at this time, or at least I don't remember coming across any, but everyone seemed to know what to do. The NCOs led their sections forward in short rushes. After a quick dash we would get down flat for a minute or two, wait a few moments and then rush forward again.

A Lewis gun team of five or six men ran past us as we lay, and I saw them fling themselves into a large, newly-made shell hole about 60 yards ahead of us. A few moments later, as I ran past, I saw the whole team lying dead in the positions they'd just taken up.

The Number One on the gun lay with his back split open from the shoulder to the waist. I was shocked, but also fascinated by the man's resemblance to a carcase in a butcher's shop.

I led several more short rushes forward and then we crossed an old 1916 trench where many others had just been killed by shell bursts. When we saw the dead we always passed them with an odd sort of detachment; this capacity to endure the sight of shattered bodies, headless trunks and detached limbs still makes me wonder.

The fact is that we accepted the war as an event in which death was almost expected and the loss of a limb was considered a lucky escape – in fact, if you were wounded badly enough to get you back to England you could be sure you would be the envy of your comrades.

Anyway, the enemy shelling eventually ceased and we began to wonder if the Germans were withdrawing their field guns. German machine-gunners certainly still held the top of the great ridge ahead of us. We were told to wait where we were while the East Yorks tried to outflank the enemy. Then the advance began again and we rushed forward to the top of the slope. As I breasted the crest and began to go downhill, bullets cracked and whined past me. Some were so close that I instinctively flinched, tucking my chin into my left shoulder as I ran even faster down the long slope before me to get it over with as quickly as possible. We had absolutely no cover and no one stopped, except those who were hit. We all tried to reach the only cover available – a big stone quarry at the bottom of the long slope.

When I got there I sat down for a moment to get my breath. Back up the long slope behind me, I could see the dead lying in twisted attitudes, but quite still and the wounded walking down. Private Neate, one of our runners, showed me his steel helmet – right in the centre of it there was a bullet hole, and in the back a jagged hole as big as a golf ball where the bullet had emerged. How Neate escaped death I'll never know.

I helped some wounded to the first-aid post which had set up shop in the shelter of the quarry. A group of German prisoners staggered by I remember, carrying some of our wounded on stretchers. I particularly noticed a young German lad, about my age, who was holding his left arm, which was soaked with his blood. He was very pale and looked appealingly at me, so I took him to the first-aid post and spoke to a corporal about him, but the corporal said, 'Those bastards will have to wait till we've seen to our own men.' Soon after this I started out again with six men and led them up the steep slope out of the quarry to a deserted road that we followed for about 100 yards. We came across a platoon of another company of Lancashire Fusiliers, and the young officer leading them asked where I was going. He got out his map and we studied it together. 'Look, Corporal,' he said, 'nobody knows what's in front of us. We'll all spread out and cross this field together.'

We left the road and advanced in a long line, each man 10 to 15 yards from the next. Soon I came to a very deep shell crater, probably made by a German howitzer. It had burst in soft soil, which was heaped round the hole, and in it were half a dozen German soldiers, some dead, some wounded. Two or three put up their hands and looked apprehensively at me. One looked as if he hadn't had a shave for a week, but the others were scared-looking boys, younger than me. I beckoned them to come up out of the shell hole, and making sure that they took no weapons with them, I pointed back the way we had come. I watched them start and then hurried on to catch up.

Daylight was fading and after sentries were posted we sat down to rest. We'd been on the go since the previous evening with neither sleep nor rations.

I managed to sleep for a time, despite the fact that it was raining. I remember I sat in the trench with my back to a grassy wall and with my steel helmet rammed into the soil to shelter my head from the rain. The map reference that the adjutant had given me and at which I was supposed to establish a post was still ahead. In fact I thought it was probably still in enemy hands.

I had not slept since the attack on Thiepval Ridge began, yet I felt guilty about sleeping. I was not under the command of the young officer and felt responsible for my six men. Two had been killed in my first attempt to carry out the vague orders I had received, but suppose I was found asleep while officially on duty in the front line! All I recall is that the night passed, nothing happened and some time later, exactly when I cannot remember, my companions and I met up with the rest of the company. No one was interested in me and my six men. The fighting had ceased for the night and next day the attack on Martinpuich was resumed. I remember advancing up a slope with shells bursting all around me, but you have to remember I was confused by hunger and fatigue so it is difficult to recollect events precisely.

I do remember watching an officer who was well in front of his company, turning back from the crest of the hill and waving and pointing to us to go to the left. Later I heard he'd seen a vast number of Germans advancing to counter-attack. We went to our left and took up a position in an old 1916 trench. It was badly damaged, but we manned the parts of it that gave us most cover, and waited to see what would happen. The shelling soon ceased and we saw movements up ahead as small groups of Germans ran along the skyline, one group carrying a heavy machine-gun. Their gun was mounted on a sledge and could easily be mistaken for a stretcher.

By this time everyone was trying to get a shot at them and several were seen to fall. The Germans had booby-trapped many of their abandoned trenches, trip-wires to hidden bombs had to be cut and all dug-outs were approached and entered with great caution. Trees had been cut down to block roads, houses in the villages had been blown up, wells had been contaminated and there were delayed action mines at crossroads.

The Germans had retreated in March 1917 to conserve manpower on a shorter and stronger line of defence, Then, just over a year later, with a million men and 5,000 guns from the collapsed Russian front, they launched their spring offensive on 21 March 1918. Six months later the Byng Boys, as we were known, were moving forward to attack on the Hindenburg Line. This grim battle was preceded by an intense and massive bombardment by our artillery. The 10th (Service) Battalion, Lancashire Fusiliers were to attack at Gouzeaucourt on the Hindenburg Line.

During the night of 17/18 September we moved into position on high ground just short of a skyline crest. While we waited a young officer came up the communication trench, looking a bit bewildered. He had just been posted to the battalion and was reporting for duty. What a time to arrive, on the eve of a great battle! The RSM questioned him, gave him some of his own rations and told him that he could not report to the company to which he had been allocated until things were more settled. The night was very still. Considering how many thousands of men were now assembled in their places all along the front, it was uncanny. Then just as it began to get light, the silence was broken by the thump of a single gun firing from behind us. Then, immediately afterwards, there was a tremendous roar of artillery as thousands of our field guns poured a ceaseless rain of shells over us into the enemy positions.

We climbed up out of our trench and stood on the top to watch. We could see the ground ahead erupting. The enemy positions were spouting smoke, soil, pieces of timber and bodies. Behind us was the ceaseless drumming of our artillery and over us, the roar and shriek of shells and the swish and flail of a storm of machine-gun bullets.

This British barrage at Gouzeaucourt on 18 September 1918 was the most intense and concentrated I experienced; the crash and thud of multiple explosions was continuous. I believe that more shells were fired on that day than on any other single day on the Western Front. The barrage was not prolonged, but it was accurate, controlled, overwhelming and unforgettable. Then it ceased, quite suddenly and there was silence. As we waited and watched, expecting the order to advance, we saw grey clad figures emerging from the black smoke in front of us and as they got nearer we could hear them coughing. They stumbled towards us with their hands up – some were wounded, all were completely dazed. We were astonished that they had managed to survive at all.

Once we'd broken through the Hindenburg Line the pace of our advance quickened. The whole front was on the move at last after four years. In 1916 and 1917, despite all the preparations, all the heroism and all the losses, the Western Front had been impassable; the machine-gun always had the last word. Now, in 1918, our field guns no longer dug in before an attack; they stood in long rows, wheel to wheel, with no cover for the gun crews. Long lines of mules with panniers, three 18 lb shells on each side, kept up the supply of ammunition. Even our company cookers moved up with us, chimneys smoking, water-carts following. A vast quantity of supplies in wagons and limbers followed close behind the advancing infantry, except when they were engaged with the enemy. On one occasion, just after the Battle of Gouzeaucourt, the battalion was issued with extra rations for forty-eight hours. They were brought up to us at night to a large farm and buildings in which we were assembling.

I was given several rockets tied up in a long heavy package encased in waterproof sheeting. They were to be used, if necessary, to signal for an artillery barrage. After that we made the most of a few hours' rest in a big old barn before the next attack. Soon after I fell asleep I was woken by the sound of a pleading voice – it was a youngster whose nerve had broken, asking to be sent down the line. As I withdrew, feeling a mixture of embarrassment and pity, I could hear the boy's pleading voice and the reassuring voice of one of the officers.

Days passed and we continued to move forward, but when we encountered them, the German troops still fought hard. They were as difficult to dislodge as ever, invariably leaving behind their tough machine-gunners to hold us up and inflict casualties until they were outflanked or otherwise forced to retreat.

There were still some costly and bloody battles to win but, by the middle of October, the British infantry, now mainly youngsters of eighteen and nineteen, were advancing far beyond that ravaged belt of country where the brutal and fruitless battles of trench warfare had raged.

The sheer scale of the final push was enormous. The follow-up of supplies, ammunition and Mills bombs, the battalions leap-frogging past one another, gave us a sense of purpose and a confidence which the men who fought in the earlier battles of 1915–17 never experienced, despite their courage and self-sacrifice.

Between 8 August and 8 November, the British Army captured 188,700 prisoners and 2,840 guns, with 350,000 casualties. Seven million men – of many nationalities – in a ceaseless battle from the Alps to the North Sea. Still men were killed routinely every day. I remember one chap called Greenhoff who was killed instantly by an exploding shell. I saw his friend hopping on one leg and waving to us. Four men left our trench and ran across the 100 yards to bring them both in; Greenhoff dead and the other lad crying, 'I'm dying, I'm dying'. We comforted him and tried to reassure him; someone spoke of the nice, clean white sheets he would soon be in, but he quickly bled to death. Little could be done in such cases; every man carried a field dressing which consisted of a pad, a bandage and a small phial of iodine, but a bad wound needed more than we could ever do. The walking wounded could usually get to a dressing station and had a good chance of early attention, but those who were taken on stretchers often had a long wait.

One Northampton man, whom I met again after the war, told me of his experiences at the casualty clearing station to which he had been carried on a stretcher. A very busy medical orderly came to him as he lay with many others waiting to be attended to and, after briefly examining his wounds, said 'You'll lose your left eye and your right hand.'

'Oh no I won't!' said my friend. 'I'm not having my hand off, I've only lost two fingers, and as for my eye, we'll see about that.'

In spite of the risk of being charged with disobeying military orders, he resisted the threat to his eye and hand. When I last saw him, in the 1940s, apart from a bad scar near his left eye and the loss of the second and third fingers of his right hand, he was very fit.

The last village we captured was Beaumont, which we entered very cautiously during the night of 10/11 November, not knowing whether the Germans were going to try to hold it, and little dreaming that the war was actually about to end. It was a very dark, cold night and the village seemed uncannily quiet as I led a group of men down the main street. A door opened for a moment and we heard a bucket overturn. We halted, rifles and bayonets at the ready. Then the door opened again, and in the light we saw a man at the bottom of a short flight of stone steps. Two women stood behind him on the stairs with the light behind them, and as we moved, they saw our uniforms and screamed, 'Les Anglais! Les Anglais!' They kept on saying it, over and over again. Then they beckoned us inside, talking excitedly all the time. They told us that the German troops had left during the evening, leaving a machine-gun rearguard at the far end of the village.

Some of our troops went on to the outskirts of the village, found no sign of the enemy and quickly returned. The women then opened an old oak chest and produced the French Tricolour. They handed round hot coffee and the old Frenchman we'd seen at the foot of the steps came into the house with a load of wood for the fire.

Later, in the half-light of dawn, I was attending to various duties as orderly sergeant, when a despatch rider rode into the village on his motor cycle and stopped to tell me that Brigade HQ had just received a special message from General Headquarters to the effect that hostilities were to cease.

The official text, as I discovered later, read:

Hostilities will cease at 1100 hours today, November 11. Troops will stand fast on the line reached at that hour. Defensive precautions will be maintained. There will be no intercourse of any description with the enemy until the receipt of instructions from GHQ.

As 11 a.m. approached, I left the village and walked back to some of our guns. The field across which I walked was littered with the usual debris of war. There were groups of German rifles, bayonets plunged into the soil, and German coal scuttle helmets hanging from them by their chin straps. I had seen this many times before and knew that they marked the hastily dug graves of our enemy in the last battle, but now it came home to me that these graves were the graves of our former enemy.

One of my strongest memories is really a rather trivial one but I mention it nonetheless. After weeks without changing your socks, you sometimes took off your boots only to discover that no socks remained. They'd disintegrated. One of the lighter mysteries of that war.

CHAPTER FIVE

EDWIN BIGWOOD

Edwin Bigwood must be one of the fittest nonagenarians in the country. At ninety-seven he has all the drive and enthusiasm of a man half his age and, apart from a slight loss of hearing caused by an operation much later in life, his experiences in the Great War left him relatively unscathed. Today he lives with his son and daughter-in-law in a quiet village near Bristol, not far from his birthplace.

When war broke out I wasn't old enough to join up, but I tried to get into the flying corps. The army wouldn't have me either, but they said if you're not old enough, put down a different age. In the end I didn't have to do that because Lord Derby brought in a scheme whereby volunteers could put their names down and as soon as they reached the age of nineteen the authorities knew they were ready to be called up.

Although it may seem strange today, at that time the idea of not trying to join up was almost unthinkable. It wasn't the fear of a white feather or the fear of being sent to Coventry it was just that this was a time when everyone wanted to be as patriotic as he or she possibly could.

Anyway, I was called up on my nineteenth birthday, 12 May 1916. I was called up into the infantry and posted to Reading, then quite a small town. From Reading I was quickly sent to join the 7th Worcestershires at Kidderminster.

I remember particularly a day when we were marching to the local baths – we did precious little other than marching in those early days. As we marched along, we passed a factory and I recall seeing all the factory girls looking out at us. And their comments! I must have led a sheltered life because I was really shocked at what they shouted at us.

After a few days in Kidderminster I was sent to the 4th Worcestershires, who were later to be virtually wiped out at Beaumont Hamel. We seemed always to be travelling in those early days and our next stop was Salisbury where, within a week, we were square-bashing and practising our bayoneting. We were given absolutely no training that had any relevance to trench warfare, which seemed odd to me later on.

On 1 July 1916 the big push started on the Somme and British losses were so enormous that we were sent to France quickly and virtually untrained. I don't remember ever being afraid when I knew we were to be sent out to France. If anything my main feeling was one of excitement. We'd all wanted to join up and now we had and we were off. It was at the end of July 1916. We went from Dover to Le Havre and then on to Rouen where men were gathered together in their thousands. We stayed here for some time and most of what went on was a revelation to me. It was another world after my quiet life near Bristol. I suppose I was really rather innocent, having always lived at home. I remember on one occasion while we waited at Rouen a rather more worldly lad who was part of our little group suggested we have a night on the town. Four of us went, I remember, and what an eye-opener that was. I will never forget it. We went to what I quickly realized was a brothel, but we had no money and I suppose we just went to gawp at the girls wearing only a slip of lace. I just couldn't believe it, but I think all four of us were really rather terrified. We had a look round and left pretty quickly. We went on to what I think was called The Red Lamp. Another establishment with no concern to conceal its true function. Here I remember we pushed the door open only to be confronted by six naked girls who rushed up to us. We were so terrified we ran away!

After yet more marching practice at Rouen we at last set off for a place called Poperinge in Belgium. It was this long march that made me realize the value of our marching training because we got to Poperinge on our feet, walking up to 20 miles a day, each of us carrying a full pack. At night when we stopped marching we simply sat down where we were, or in the nearest trench, and fell asleep in our clothes and packs. That's how tired we were.

The first night I slept like this I woke with a start after a few hours and took off my pack. Straight away I saw a hole in it and I just couldn't understand how on earth I'd managed to cut it open like that. Then I discovered that while I'd slept a rat had bitten its way into my pack and eaten all my rations. After that I soon learned that you had to keep your wits about you just to keep ahead of the rats, let alone the Germans!

Life in the trenches was very bad, but we were not to know just how bad for a while. From Poperinge we set off to Goudicourt – a very long way. In fact I felt so bad after one particularly long day that I thought I was going to have to drop out. I sat at the side of the road and a medic came along and said what's wrong. I said I was exhausted but he made me get up and carry on. I was simply made to get back on my feet and back into line. There was no question of doing anything else, however exhausted I was. I remember at the end of one long day's march we stopped at the top of a hill before dismiss for the night. I was waiting for our tents to arrive – I assumed we'd be sleeping in the standard army bell tents – so I asked the sergeant-major who simply said, 'What bloody tents?' He then said if you don't like the wind, dig a hole.

The Battle of the Somme was certainly my most terrible experience, although I was to be part of the war from July 1916 to January 1918. We had to go over the top after the usual pulverizing barrage of shells, which of course, as we know now, was at best only partly effective. I don't remember the exact date but I remember an officer blowing a whistle and then we went over. It was as simple and as terrifying as that. Then the artillery started and, of course, that was the wrong way round. The artillery should have been firing before we went over. As soon as we were visible the Germans opened fire. There were people falling and dying absolutely everywhere. Many were half killed or badly injured. It was chaos. An officer who was badly injured in the stomach asked me to take a message so, through the very thick of the battle, I went with a young lad and we held hands and ran through the shell fire. God knows how we escaped being hit amid that carnage, but we ran back to the support line past men screaming for us to help them. Some begged us to cut their legs or arms off. The bodies and screams were the stuff of eternal nightmares.

The next thing I remember is being on the top of a hill back at the support line when a shell exploded nearby. It was a huge explosion and we were buried completely in mud and rubble. We were dug out fairly quickly but it doesn't take long for your muscles to be crushed in such a way that you find it impossible to move for hours. I was okay but it took two hours before I could walk again. The men who'd been on either side of me when the shell exploded were killed outright.

Soon after this we went through Delville Wood. We called it Devil's Wood. An officer went on up ahead of us and we could hear the whistle of bullets. I was a Lewis gunner and followed the officer up to a ridge. I peered over and on the other side there were dozens of Germans who had no idea we were approaching. I raked them with fire till I ran out of ammunition. You just didn't think about it. I massacred them until I had no ammunition left. By this time the other men had reached my position. I was so elated that, in a moment of madness, I borrowed a rifle from another soldier and started picking off the few remaining Germans who were still alive. Of course the

Germans were firing back at us the whole time and I could feel the bullets whistling round my feet, but I never suffered even a scratch and I was fully exposed the whole time. After a few moments of firing I said to one of my friends, 'You have a try.' So he took the rifle, stood up and was killed instantly with a bullet through the head.

The next battle I remember well was at Monchy Le Pru. Here we'd taken a ridge, but before we knew where we were the Germans counter-attacked. We ran out of ammunition and I could see Germans chasing our men with bayonets, but there was nothing anyone could do. We scratched around in the chalk and dust under our feet in a desperate attempt to find a few shells, but with no luck. Right in the middle of this nightmare a young man came up to me and said, 'Is your name Bigwood?' I said yes and he replied 'Well, mine's Smallwood.' Such a funny exchange in the middle of a savage battle, but the war produced odd bits of humour like that because when we were in trenches our time was spent mostly being bored. Only now and then when there was a battle or shelling would we be terrified for what, I suppose, were really relatively short periods — short compared to the long periods of inactivity anyway.

I can remember what I think must have been the world's first ever tank battle. It was at Cambrai. Tanks had been used before Cambrai but in isolation and they were therefore easy for the enemy to pick off. I remember following a tank with my machine-gun. It got to the top of a trench and proceeded in a few seconds to kill every German in sight. Behind us and in the wake of the tank were some 1,000 cavalry ready to consolidate what we'd taken.

Another tank tried to cross a canal and I can recall watching it crash down through the bridge into the water, Still, we were able to use the tank as a new bridge since there was no way of getting it going again. At Cambrai I remember the locals came out of their houses to see our tanks. I asked one of them for water and he gave us wine! That was a rather wonderful moment. An officer shouted at us as we drank it, 'Don't you realize there's a war on.' That was a bit rich considering we'd been there for a year by then. After Cambrai I did fatigue duties for a while – mostly carrying barbed wire endlessly to the front line.

In winter our trenches were unbelievable. The mud would get softer and softer and, after a storm, we would often be waist deep in sludge. Many men suffered from hernias as a result of straining just to lift their legs out of it to move a few yards.

My last battle was Passchendaele. Everywhere was deep in mud and I was still carrying barbed wire. As I ran along I suddenly felt a hot searing pain in my face. 'I've got a blighty,' I shouted. Seems a funny reaction now, but I was so elated that I was only half scared. I was bleeding so fast that my wound had to be dressed immediately and I was given an escort to get me back to a casualty station. We stumbled along the duck-boards till we reached a crossroads. Then my escort said we had to go to the right. I thought it was left and that was the way I insisted we go, which was just as well really because he was wrong as it turned out and I was losing blood fast.

I was virtually unconscious when I reached the casualty station, but I made it. They sent me to Etaples, which had the biggest hospital in the whole war area. Here my innocence got me in trouble again. I couldn't get out of bed so the nurse gave me a bed bottle which I used and then hung on to for about five hours not knowing what I was supposed to do with it. I thought that if I put it on the floor it would spill everywhere. The nurses thought this was very funny.

After some days I was taken in a horse-drawn ambulance to Calais to catch the Dover boat, but by this time the wound in my face had made it set rigid. I couldn't even open my mouth. I was terrified that if the river crossing was rough and I felt sick I would drown in my own vomit! I made up my mind that the best thing would be to sleep, which is exactly what I did. I was then sent to Sheffield Lunatic Asylum of all places. I was there for five months and then spent the next twelve years trying to get my weight above

8 stone without much success. And it took years to get rid of the severe chest infections I'd suffered from in the trenches.

In some ways it was the daily routine in the trenches that prevented the soldiers going mad. Every morning we had to stand to at dawn. Imagine that. All along the hundreds of miles of trenches every morning millions of soldiers standing on their fire-steps for an hour. After that we'd have breakfast if there was anything. If you were in a bad place for deliveries you might get water brought up in old petrol cans and it tasted so foul as a result that you couldn't drink it. If it was really bad – and we always seemed to be desperately short of water – you might have to try drinking out of a shell hole. That could be very dangerous if there were traces of gas in the water – you could get severely burned. For the rest, our rations were mostly bully beef and dog biscuits – but that was at bad times. If things were reasonable we might get bread and jam, tea, sugar and condensed milk and, of course, cigarettes. These were always one of three brands: Cinderella, Woodbine or Ruby Reds. We'd perhaps get five or ten cigarettes a day. Then, after breakfast, we'd sit around talking and being bored unless of course any action was planned or imminent or we were under fire. I remember a new officer arrived one day and asked me what my bit of trench was like. He would have been about twenty-one. I said everything was pretty quiet and he simply said, 'Well, I'll have a look for myself.' I tried to tell him it was very dangerous but he wouldn't listen. He climbed over the top of the trench, went about 50 yards and was shot dead.

In the bitter winter of 1916/17 some of the trenches had coke braziers in them and the men would try all sorts of things to get near the heat. If you were stuck on the outside of the circle of men round a brazier you might throw some cartridges into the fire to get everyone to run away long enough to gain you a place right up near the front.

The whole war was actually organized chaos. With so many men and animals and all the complicated back-up such a huge operation needed, we were always getting lost or men from one regiment would get mixed up with the men from another. I fell asleep by a brazier one night only to discover the next day that I hadn't a clue where I was or where my own men were!

In the long years since the war ended I've often thought I must be a very callous man. I killed so many men without really thinking anything of it. It was just something you had to do. And I think that if you worried about it you were finished. You wouldn't have lasted five minutes.

And whatever people say to the contrary, there was no let up at Christmas. There would be a new draft of men and we would learn some new songs from home from them. That was about it.

In 1916 we didn't even have tin hats and our gas masks were simple felt hoods with a tube sticking out, through which you were supposed to breathe.It wasn't until 1917 that the new box respirators arrived. Mind you, I don't think they were much good either.

I was twice recommended for bravery awards. An officer told me I deserved to get them but there were only enough medals for officers and NCOs. At that time you could tell someone something like that and it was just accepted. There was still a real sense that social class made the kind of difference that justified that kind of statement. I remember, too, a colonel once saying, 'I've got a batch of medals. They've just arrived. Who shall I give them to?' He was told that Major so-and-so had been out for two years so let's give him one. He got the DSO. That sort of thing was just the way it was.

The memory that stays with me most, and it has always haunted me, is the sound of the wounded at the Battle of the Somme. The air was filled with their pitiful screams, but there were too many for us to help. They were everywhere. Doctors tried to tend to them on the battlefield, but so many doctors had been killed that the few remaining could not hope to cope. When we walked over the top at the Somme – and we'd been given instructions not to run, but to walk in a discliplined line – it was amazing we weren't all killed. We were just big, easy, standing targets given to the Germans to mow down. On the first day more than 30 per cent of us were killed or injured. And as I walked towards the enemy trenches at the Somme, men were blown up and killed time and time again right next to me, yet I never gave it a second thought. Lots of the men took hours to die. Hours. Your chances of being helped or put out of your misery were much reduced, too, if you were hit in the evening because that meant you would almost certainly be out all night.

The men *did* think the generals were to blame. They didn't really know what they were doing and the idea that a man should be proud to die for his country was so strong in their minds that they really thought thousands dead was a mere detail. Earl Haig was undoubtedly incompetent. He was too old and stuck in his ways. He'd been brought up on the Boer War and the lessons of that war were useless in the Great War.

Though I'm sure they would not have admitted it, the generals' attitude was undoubtedly conditioned by the fact that, personally, their lives were never at risk. They were as far removed from us as the Prince of Wales who once rode by the trenches to review the troops. He just saw numberless men and rode on.

CHAPTER SIX

GEORGE JAMESON

George Jameson is exactly one hundred years old. He was born in Newcastle upon Tyne on December 19 1892 and started work at Armstrong Whitworth's, the battleship builders, at the age of sixteen. His family had lived in the north-east for generations – his grandfather was made a freeman of the city of Berwick-upon-Tweed. George was educated at Dame Alleyn's Catholic School where he developed two great loves: horses and ships. Looking back more than eighty years, he is still enthusiastic about his early interests and about the way in which his early years moulded his character. A quite remarkably fit man who moves and smiles easily and whose voice has a bell-like clarity with only a few traces of his Newcastle accent, George is one of the very last of the 'Old Contemptibles'. When I met him in his memento-filled flat in the pretty Devon seaside town of Sidmouth, he took me back, first, to his early days in the smoke-filled city of Newcastle.

As I was mostly interested in ships and horses and as there was little money to be made from any business I could do that was connected with horses, it was intended that I should go to Durham University as part of an indented apprenticeship at Armstrong's. I was to become a naval architect, which is why I left school at sixteen to start my three years.

Armstrong's was fascinating at this time – about 1908 – because they still had a wooden ship, *The Calliope*, which was used as a training aid along with the ordnance and the steelworks.

When war broke out I'd already done four years in the territorial army. Many of my friends joined the Northumberland Hussars – one of only two territorial units to have served in the South African War. The great attraction of the Hussars, of course, was that you got a horse. So, as soon as I got the chance, I switched to the Northumberland Hussars. Peter Cook was our commander in chief and I remember he went to the War Office to get us a job! We assembled eventually at Gosforth Park on 14 August 1914. By September we'd come to Lyndhurst in Hampshire, where the 7th Division was being assembled. The 7th Division was a crack regular division and we were appointed divisional cavalry. We used to ask the regulars if they were worried at the idea that they were being guarded on their flanks by us – a bunch of rookies. We liked to tease them, but I don't think they were too bothered.

On 5 October 1914 we sailed for Zeebrugge, but this took much longer than it should have done because we fiddled about, worried by submarines. The idea was that the 7th Division should relieve the naval division penned in at Antwerp, but by the time we arrived the naval division had surrendered to the Germans so we went on through Bruges to Ypres. We were at the first Battle of Ypres. In fact, we, the cavalry, were nursing brigade after brigade through Belgium to Ypres and we had a brush or two with the enemy on the way.

In the cloth hall at Ypres there is a photograph of the regiment arriving in the square and I can still make out several colleagues – and myself – in that picture. We were forming up in the square at the time. Every man kept his own horse in the cavalry and we were trained to protect the flanks of a body of men.

We arrived at Ypres on 13 October. The infantry were moving up and we were told that Ypres had to be held at whatever cost because it was the gateway to the Channel ports. The men involved in the struggle to hold Ypres became known as the 'Old Contemptibles' because that was how the Kaiser once referred to us. He said that we were a contemptible little army that would be swept into the sea by his forces.

I remember the infantry were digging in around the front at Ypres and one day my troop officer told me to take my patrol up to the Menin Gate and find some Germans! All we found was a massive chateau and we were so hungry we decided to have a look inside for food. We didn't find a scrap to eat but we did find masses of champagne so we got rather tipsy on that. While we were in the chateau it was being bumped around rather badly by shells and I remember two small bronze medallions fell off one of the walls. One showed the cloth hall at Ypres, the other showed a man called Edward Pecker. I took those medallions and carried them right through the war. They are now back in the chateau which has been rebuilt twice. We tried to find out who Pecker was, perhaps the owner of the chateau, but with no luck.

My war actually nearly finished in the first week. I'll tell you how it happened. I was standing one day holding a small group of horses in Sanctuary Wood. The wood was being shelled but nothing had fallen particularly close to me and I was vaguely reassured by the presence of the infantry who were trickling through as they made their way forward. We were preparing the breakthrough that never came. Anyway, shells were falling all around as I say, when the chap next to me asked if I had a light. I said yes and offered him one. At that instant a shell fell right on top of us, or that's the way it seemed. The man to whom I'd offered the light was killed instantly and my horse was split open from one end to the other. My greatcoat, which had been rolled on the saddle, had a great big piece of shrapnel in it.

In spite of the horrors of the following weeks we held Ypres in the end but of the 15,000 in the division fewer than 5,000 men were left when we were relieved on 5 November.

We were there for just over a month and at one time during that period there was such a shortage of manpower that everyone was ordered up to the line – cooks, bottle-washers, everyone. I remember being sent back to bring up the reserve and that was significant because the reserve I went to collect was the last there was!

At the beginning of the first Battle of Ypres the whole army was commanded by cavalry generals and at Mons and many other battles the cavalry were always used. It must have been unthinkable for the men who commanded us not to use the cavalry. We supported the division, although at Ypres we were also used in the trenches. When the first division was in the line we – the cavalry – were used to transport messages. But the horror of the trenches at this time for all the men was that we were outnumbered by the Germans by about five to one. Our training in the use of musketry was so magnificent, however, that the Germans often thought we had six machine-guns where we actually had one.

By the time I reached Loos nearly fifteen months later we'd left our horses behind. At Loos we relieved the Grenadier Guards who were much, much taller than we were. I went on leave at about this time and I remember that I'd decided I really only wanted to be in the cavalry. I didn't like infantry work at all. I tried to get a commission and when I returned to France and was sent up into the line I remember one September day being told to get myself smartened up to go to see Divisional General Watts. He treated me very kindly. I was approved for a commission and approved to go back to Britain. On 15 December I was commissioned in the 1st Northumberland Brigade, the 50th Division, and I spent a month at the Edinburgh School of Gunnery.

From Edinburgh I went to Ripon where all the mounted regiments were trained. I was there until 1916 and then returned to France. By July or early August of that year I was at a place called Clyte, just in front of Mount Camel. Then my division, the 50th, went on to the Somme at High Wood. The artillery was concentrated just where I was and it was quite incredible. The guns were lined up hub to hub and the shelling from them was so intense and so continual that if you touched the barrels you'd lose the skin off your hands. In fact they got so hot that the copper binding strips used to come off a shell every now and then and when it was fired it would go completely haywire, somersaulting through the air and exploding prematurely. So many shells were going from our side over to the German lines that we built walls behind our position in case a premature shell from our own side should come down on us from behind.

What used to happen with the shelling was that after initial bombardment the top brass would meet and decide when the attack would begin. The whole thing had to be carefully synchronized because after so many minutes of artillery fire everything would fall silent, the guns would be re-aimed to a position 150 yards further forward and then our infantry would move up to where the shelling had previously been aimed. Obviously the aim was to damage the enemy so badly at a certain point ahead of us that when our men went forward they would not come under attack.

Thus the pattern would be artillery fire, followed by artillery fire moving forward 150 yards, followed by our men moving up again. As a signaller my job was to keep communications going. We had to get into position in support of an advancing line of men in order that we could send signals back so the artillery would know where to aim their fire. In a sense we were the eyes and ears of the generals at the place where the battle was actually taking place. So if, for example, we were in the front line and our advance had been halted by a machine-gun forward of us and on the left, I would signal back the position of the gun and our artillery would try to knock it out. It was a particularly terrifying sort of job because you were often in the midst of fighting men who could at least fire back, but as a signaller you had merely to take note of everything happening around you and report back. You couldn't do a thing in terms of the actual combat.

After a tremendous artillery barrage, the Battle of the Somme started in July 1916 and, in fact, it really went on more or less till the end of the war. At the Somme, land was taken and then re-taken, lost and gained in an endless shifting pattern. The real breakthrough didn't come until 1917/18. Until then it was just bits of land, scraps almost, that were endlessly fought over, lost and gained, lost and gained.

I remember one night we were waiting at the front line. We were ordered to move forward. There was no movement at all ahead of us so we began. Astonishingly we encountered no Germans at all. As it happened we discovered later that they'd silently fallen back that night from a series of winding trenches to a nice straight trench that had complete command of the whole area as it ran along much higher ground – this was the Hindenburg Line.

Major conflicts since the Great War have been so different in terms of how they were organized that it is difficult now to understand exactly what it was like for the individual soldier between 1914–18. Apart from during specific battles – and these lasted a relatively short time, though they were incredibly intense – you could be killed or injured at any moment wherever you were at the front. By that I mean you could be killed even if you were in one of the reserve trenches because these areas were covered by searching and sweeping enemy fire and, of course, they were regularly shelled, day and night. Our reserve trenches would be under attack from the German rear positions. In some ways you were in far more danger further back from the front – this was true even if you were 1,000 yards back. Here shrapnel from shells could get you and there were planes coming over all the time from the German side to check on the disposition of our men so *you* knew *they* knew where you were and that they'd pretty soon send over some shells to see if they could kill you.

One particularly nasty episode I remember occurred when the Canadians were given the job of capturing Vimy Ridge. The

British and French had already tried to take it but without success. The Canadians told the British they wanted the best fire power we could muster before they went forward. We were using mobile army brigades and they were being shunted all over the place. I was with one of these and we were attached to the Canadians when they tried – and succeeded – in taking Vimy. The weather was absolutely appalling at the time of that offensive. In fact, it was so bad that the top brass thought about calling it off – and for them to even think about that, things really did have to be terrible. Before the battle began we had to get forward across the filthy shell-pocked muddy ground. The infantry were used to drag our guns through the mire, weaving around the shell holes and around the dead horses and men. We got as far forward as the old German line which was roughly 100 yards from the crest of Vimy Ridge itself. Once the Germans had been driven back their heavy guns began pounding and to avoid them we continually moved 100 yards to the left and then 100 yards to the right. We were trying to work out the right barrages to cover our infantry, particularly on the right. All this happened at night with the rain lashing down, mud everywhere, shells bursting and the desperate attempt always to keep some order amid the chaos. I remember one chap, a tall fellow from South America, known to us all as Husky Jake, grabbed a pair of gumboots and vanished into the night. We thought that he was done for – drowned in a shell hole or killed by shrapnel. An hour later he came back completely soaked and covered in mud. He was still carrying the gumboots so we asked why he hadn't worn them. The answer, and it seemed so tragically funny at the time, was simply that once outside he'd realized they didn't fit but he'd hung on to them anyway.

Most battles, and this one for Vimy Ridge was no exception, had to develop according to what happened as and when the fighting started and continued. Here the Germans had the high ground which was a nuisance for us; another time we might be in a trench loop and get caught in cross fire from the two sides of that loop.

Everything in a battle was based on working out a series of objectives. Then the barrage would come down to prepare the ground and to allow the infantry to go forward in bounds.

The confusion of a battle could be worrying too. For example, one part of our forward line might break through the enemy line and they might end up cut off and on their own surrounded by the enemy if we didn't break through anywhere else. If there was a particularly troublesome area we might have to concentrate our men to attack that part of the line and, of course, in doing that we might make another part of our line vulnerable. Going over the top early on in the war was a messy business. It would start as a kind of orderly procession but quickly become very messy indeed. The officers leading an advance would have pre-timed their moves, or estimated them at least. So as the men moved forward they knew they had to drop into set positions. Having reached a particular tree stump or shell hole they would stop, wait for the artillery to start up and hammer their next objective and then move forward again when the artillery had stopped. As far as possible a line of men moving forward had to be as solid as possible, because that was the only way it would retain the ability to repel an attack. That was the ideal, of course, but in the confusion of battle it didn't always work out like that. Of one thing we could always be sure, however; every battle eventually came to a standstill. Sometimes we gained our objective, sometimes not. If we didn't gain our objective we'd have to retreat and improvise a new position further back. Once we'd taken Vimy Ridge and we were at the top of it we had the whole of the Plain of Arras in front of us, stretching away into the distance.

It was a great observation position because you could see so far ahead, but as we were on top of the only raised ground for miles we were also the perfect target for a hell of a hammering. By the time Vimy Ridge had been taken we'd been hammered and pinned down in the same place for so long that, together with a group of friends, I decided to risk it and go for a walk. Sounds an odd thing to do, but we just needed to move around after the tension of such a long battle. We walked down the face of the ridge and then thought why not drag our guns down – this was really a bit cheeky because it was too far forward for a gun position. We found some people to come down with stakes and camouflage material, then six guns were brought down. It was very difficult to move the guns – one man had to hang right over the muzzle while two dragged the thing which twisted and slithered in the blackness, but in terms of our safety we were much better off down the ridge than at the top.

Our infantry were holding the line ahead of us and when the German counter-attack came as it always did after we'd gained some ground, it was savage, incredibly savage and sustained. They did their absolute damnedest to take the ground back from us. We were firing from our position at the bottom of our ridge when we discovered that the German counter-attack had been successful on our right flank. We couldn't put lines of fire down ahead of us until we discovered exactly which shell holes our men were in. At this stage there was a great deal of confusion with the line having been broken in at least one place by the Germans. Our brass didn't know where the men were so I was asked to crawl forward and take a look. I should add, at this point, that sometimes we created a new forward trench by digging in such a way as to join up a series of shell holes. Anyway, at this stage during the Vimy Ridge counter-attack we were very close to the front for a field battery and it was essential that we try to find out as much as possible about the exact state of the line. So that night I crawled out and simply made a sketch of how the front seemed. I made the sketch on a message pad as best I could under the circumstances. A runner then took this back so the gunners would know where to fire to protect the front line. Each time our front line moved forward we had to get a wire to the new forward position wherever that happened to be. At one stage during the counter-attack we could actually see the Germans coming towards us – a young subaltern gave me a gun and some grenades, but I told him I had to keep the wires going because it was only by signalling back across the wires that I was able to direct our fire in such a way as to destroy the enemy advance. On that occasion the infantry brigadier thanked me for my help.

The whole of the First World War in the trenches depended on telephone wire. It was the best form of signalling we had, but it was also extremely vulnerable to being broken by enemy shells and mortars. In fact, this is what made the linesman's job so dangerous – he was the one who had to get out there whatever the conditions and repair any damage to the wire. After stopping the counter-attack at Vimy Ridge I recommended a number of my linesmen for medals.

From Vimy Ridge we eventually moved north toward Arras. We fought at Neuport where we'd been sent to rest after the Battle of Vimy Ridge, but the Germans gassed us there so our rest turned into another battle. In fact we were well plastered at Neuport because we couldn't dig deep enough trenches. The water table was too high and our trenches were so shallow that the gunners behind us had to build barriers in front of their positions to protect us from our own fire.

It was here that an infantryman near me suddenly spotted an aeroplane high over our heads. It was a German plane and they were taking photographs of our positions. The infantry asked us to help so we went off and found a horse-drawn hay buggy that we then turned into a gun platform by placing it in a gun pit. We cocked the gun's nose into the air and regulated it on the front line using the air burst of shells. When the trap was set we knew we had a chance of only two, or at most three shots. When the plane came back over we scared the pants off the crew I'm sure – our troops were delighted even though we didn't actually hit the plane, but it came back a great deal higher after that and there was nothing else we could do.

Most of us escaped death by inches on numerous occasions, and I was very slighty hurt in the leg on one occasion. Other than that

I escaped without a scratch, although I was conscious of some really narrow escapes. North of Arras, for example, we were firing our guns to support the guards who were in the front line. I was at the back of our gun with a whistle and a watch. As I blew the whistle the guns would increase their range and the guards could go forward. Unfortunately a German battery had spotted the flashes from our gun and they began shelling us. One shell hit and killed a complete gun crew 70 yards from my position and a piece of shrapnel came whizzing along and hit me on my tin hat. It cut the steel band that went round the hat and then spun into my face, cutting it slightly – an inch or two higher or lower and it would have killed me.

At High Wood Ridge one freezing winter, I think it might have been 1914, I was walking away from the front when I heard a shell coming over. I was a seasoned soldier by then and knew when a shell was going to come close or land far enough away for safety. This one I knew was going to be very close, but I hadn't anticipated exactly how close. It landed within a couple of feet of me, skidded on the frozen ground, bounced back up into the air and exploded 100 yards further on. There is absolutely no doubt at all that had the ground been softer that shell would have exploded on impact and I would have been killed instantly.

On another occasion, at Vimy Ridge I think it was, we were in the process of pulling out of the line one gun team at a time. We were loading up odd bits and pieces of kit on to a horse-drawn general service wagon when we heard a shell coming. It landed under one of the four horses and failed to explode. Again, had it exploded when it should there would have been little left of me.

Another time some friends and I were walking back from the front line past a communications trench when we thought we'd walk along the top. It was a sunny, relatively peaceful afternoon. As we went along we suddenly heard an aeroplane coming close and unfortunately for us it was a German plane. We felt like rabbits. As the noise of the approaching plane grew louder we scattered in all directions, but already machine-gun bullets were spattering everywhere. You had to keep jinking in a desperate attempt to avoid being hit, but the least bit of bad luck and that would have been it anyway. He came round again and had another go, but we were all lucky and no one was hit.

From October 1917 until early 1918 I was in Italy at Piave. Here we had to stop the Germans getting across the river, but as it turned out we didn't fire a shot. The only bit of excitement we had was when we were ordered to organize a raid to collect prisoners after a battery – in other words after our guns had softened the enemy up.

Before we could hope to carry out the raid effectively we had to deal with some enemy searchlights, so I took a couple of guns up on to a hill and we fused some shells at about the right range for the German searchlights. I got the guns in position, but the instant our barrage started it began snowing heavily and the whole thing was called off. We weren't having any of that so we decided to shoot out the German searchlights anyway and we did it. But we were really there – in Italy I mean – just in case the Germans managed to break through the line.

In the end, when the German breakthrough did come, it was spring 1918, and it wasn't in Italy but in France. We were rushed back to the Western Front and I fought in various actions there. Once we'd stopped the German onslaught they were pushed back and kept in almost continuous retreat. It was only then after so many long years that we were able to move forward out of the trenches and into open country. The German offensive had worked initially because it pushed us back, but the vital point is that although it pushed our line back it didn't break it. They just couldn't get through and when they eventually retreated they didn't have time to get back into their trenches. We had them on the run as it were. The problem for the Germans was that they got too far ahead of themselves. They were too far ahead of their ammo and supplies and as a result, when they retreated, they retreated very quickly. As we went forward, pushing hard against the retreating enemy, we still lost men and horses every day. I remember on one occasion at about this time we came across a big stable full of dead horses, but open war, war away from the trenches, was much better and, of course, morale was high because we were moving so rapidly. We advanced several miles every day.

We supported the New Zealanders at a place called Le Quesnoy, a village with ancient encircling walls 12 ft thick. We were passing this place when a soldier told us to get down in a ditch as there was a German gunner on the parapet of the wall. We were wondering what to do about this when a soldier saw a note plastered on a fence post which said that as from 11 a.m. that day all hostilities were to cease. Had we gone along that road and not got down into the ditch the German gunner might have finished us off just when the war was ending.

My worst memory of the whole war is of the beginning. Once I'd become a battery officer I was in danger, but at least I could get washed now and then, life was better and I knew a little more about survival and battle and what was going on generally. As an ordinary soldier I hadn't a clue about anything outside my own small area of concern.

In 1914 the Kaiser had contemptuously said he would sweep us into the sea – this was at Ypres – and we had a very bad time. Our whole area was under a constant, dense bombardment of shells – you couldn't move even a few yards and when the battle was at its height I was sent back with a message to alert a division in reserve. I remember that on my way back I had to cross the square at Ypres and there were dead horses everywhere and a terrible stench of death. The great cloth hall was damaged and it was pouring with rain. I managed to get my horse, but almost as soon as I'd gone any distance on him he went lame so I left him in a field. I soon found a bicycle but I got bogged down in the thick mud that lay everywhere. Shells were coming down just about everywhere too, and I was completely soaked, but I had to keep on walking. What else could I do? I was seriously wondering if I had any chance of surviving but somehow I managed. I discovered, too, that a despatch rider with the same message had already got to where I was supposed to be going. Two messengers were usually sent with the same message in a battle just in case one didn't make it. I got back eventually, found a zinc bath in a shed and fell asleep in it totally exhausted.

For someone who's never been in a battle it must seem terrible to be surrounded by the dead and the dying. Well, it is certainly true that seeing someone killed right in front of your eyes is a terrible thing, but it happened so often and there was nothing anyone could do about it. One particularly unpleasant weapon the Germans used was the *Minnenwerfer*. These things were so nasty that we always posted sentries specifically to look for them coming towards our position. They were big mortars filled with scrap metal and would literally blow a trench to pieces. Luckily, they made a very easily identifiable noise as they flew through the air, so we could usually hear them coming.

Our stretcher-bearers were marvellously brave men. Whatever the circumstances they went out immediately to pick up the wounded men. They had to be under fire like everyone else but they couldn't fight back as they didn't carry rifles and they couldn't take avoiding action if they were to help the wounded.

At Loos, during the second phase of the whole show, we were sent to pull out some German guns and a very good friend of mine was badly injured just in front of me as he started to move them. They'd been booby trapped and he lost part of his foot.

There were occasions, too, when things were so bad that the wounded could not be collected. That was terrible. I remember one friend lay out injured all night in no man's land. He was hit again during the night when a shell exploded quite close to him but, amazingly, he survived.

When I returned to England after the war I'd been mentioned in dispatches and I had a Military Cross. There was no work in shipbuilding by the time I returned, but through a friend of my girlfriend's father, a millionaire coal owner, I got a job looking after the office of an inventor. I ran his office in Pilgrim Street, Newcastle upon Tyne, but it was a pretty insecure business and just after getting married I lost the job. I then went to London and studied for the Institute of Chartered Secretaries exam. I became a chartered secretary and eventually got a job as company secretary at an engineering works in Letchworth, Hertfordshire. I joined in 1932 and stayed for twenty years. During the Second World War we helped build tanks for the western desert and submarines so I suppose that you could say that I returned at last to naval engineering.

George Jameson was already serving with the army when war broke out in 1914

Horses were used throughout the Great War to transport men and supplies

A pontoon-bridge section pulled by a four-hourse team

Fully-trained recruits of the 7th Battalion, the West Kents, including Oliver Andrews (standing, far right), pose for a formal group picture at Fleet in Essex in 1915

Oliver Andrews (left) photographed just behind the front line with a friendly French farmer and his son who was fighting with the French army

Tom Broach, a photograph he carried with him during the long months in the trenches

Basil Farrer

Blacksmiths at the front were essential to the war effort

"What time do they feed the sea lions Alf"

A cartoon drawn by Capt. Bruce Bairnsfather, from More Fragments from France, *a popular magazine of the day aimed specifically at soldiers serving at the front*

Publications aimed at soldiers tried to keep up moral with lighthearted cartoons like these: 'The Professional Touch – "Chuck us out that bag o' bombs, mate: it's under your 'ead"'

'Those superstitions – Private Sandy McNab cheers the assembly by pointing out (with the aid of his pocket almanac) that it is Friday the 13th and that their number is one too many'

Scenes of devastation: above: the remains of the church and Central Street in Assevillers on the Somme; below: the village of Herbécourt lies in ruins

Two visions from the inferno: above: the entrance to the village of Estrées; below: the town of Albert after the bombardment on the Somme

The ruins of the church at Albert

854 ⁰ EUROPEAN WAR 1914-1917. — Ham... merican journalist mission in front of t... Castle... on journaliste américaine devant le Château.-LL

American journalists visit the front at Hamil after the end of the war

CHAPTER SEVEN

GRANT OSBORNE

After suffering a stroke at the age of ninety-two, the Reverend Grant Osborne made a rapid recovery much to the astonishment of doctors at the local hospital where he was treated. Indeed, his return to a full and active life was so swift that he was taken around the wards and held up as an example to encourage much younger stroke patients to believe that they too could make a full recovery. His battling spirit and refusal to give in probably also explain his remarkable longevity, as I discovered when I went to visit him in the pretty Norfolk Broads village of Hoveton where he lives with his daughter. A dapper figure with an almost boyish smile, he talks readily and with great animation about his youth and his days fighting in France.

I was born in a place with a long naval tradition – Portland in Dorset. Throughout my boyhood and youth my father served in the old Naval fleet. He was always away on some distant sea and because the fleet was based either at Portland or at Portsmouth down the coast, we were constantly on the move back and forth between one place and the other. As always in the army or the Navy, wives would follow their husbands and so my mother followed my father. As a result my education was rather confused to say the least! I was never in one school long enough to find out what was what. But my father had been quite old when I was born – or that's how it seemed then – and by the time I reached my early teens he had retired and we moved to Redhill, which was then a very quiet village in Surrey.

When eventually I left school – it would have been almost exactly three years before the outbreak of war in 1914 – I went to work with a coachbuilder. Well, more precisely I was apprenticed to a coachbuilder which was how most people started work in those days. I can just remember helping with the work on some big mahogany and brass ambulances. Every town in the country had one of these and of course vehicle bodywork was done by companies who had made – and were still making – coaches and carriages to be drawn by horses. It was still rare to see a motor vehicle in those days, very rare in some places.

Anyway, these great wooden ambulances were most beautifully made, although I doubt if any have survived. All coachwork, whether for motorized or horse-drawn transport, had the same kind of hand-built bodies – we were sent the chassis of the vehicle, we drew up plans for the body and then we built it. I'd been at the coachworks – they were called Chalmers & Co. – for about three years and I was getting on quite well. I don't think I was brilliant or anything but I remember I entered a competition and won a prize for my design for a taxi-cab.

When talk of war began my father was quickly called up. Soon after that my mother and I went back down to Portland for a holiday and we were still there when war was declared. It was a Tuesday I think, but it was hard to imagine at that stage that the war would have any real effect on our lives. At the end of the first week of hostilities we went back to Redhill and I returned to Chalmers. We had a big job on at that time building five charabancs. When I'd left to go on holiday they were nearly ready, when I got back a week later all the seats had been taken out of them and they'd been requisitioned as army vehicles.

I was sent a badge to wear which said that I was involved in essential munitions work because we made artillery wheels, general service wagons and so on. I think the government knew that patriotism being what it was at that time no young man would have stayed put unless he had to – and they were telling us in no uncertain terms that we were staying put. Hence the badges. They needed the equipment and we had the skills to make it.

I remember that summer of 1914 because of the endless, glorious sunshine. It was a quite brilliant summer and as the weeks wore on we were ordered to build ten general service wagons. These were used to carry equipment and supplies. We'd never seen one before so the ministry sent us a full size wagon and a series of drawings from which to work – the wagon was so enormous we couldn't fit it in the workshop! In those days craftsmen really were craftsmen and every detail of the drawings was checked – even the screws were drawn to scale.

Although I wasn't yet part of the war I felt as though I was because our work had changed so much and there was a permanent sense of urgency. When the army wanted us to build vehicles they always wanted them quickly. I think the fact that I've always had bad eyes stems from this time because the brilliant sunshine reflected so brightly through the workshop windows on to the white paper of the drawings.

Most of my friends had been called up by this time but because of my work I wasn't allowed to join up. There was such a feeling of patriotism too at the time that men in civilian clothes were constantly being harassed by women and girls – sometimes very young girls. Some girls where I lived got very uppish with me and said that I was afraid to go to the war. They really did go around handing out white feathers and it was terribly embarrassing to receive one. I suppose it was simply that that was the morality of the time. King and country and duty were accepted uncritically.

I got so fed up with the jibes and the white feathers that in spite of my essential war work badge I went along to my local recruiting office in an attempt to join up. I was immediately told to get out. In fact they almost shouted at me. I tried on numerous occasions to join up after that first attempt but all to no avail. My munitions work made it impossible and they didn't care about the girls with their white feathers!

This went on fairly unsatisfactorily until not long before the Battle of the Somme. At that time there was a great rush of men and eventually I was accepted as a private. I was more astonished than anybody and I have to admit I was also delighted. That was the remarkable thing – can you imagine someone these days being delighted at the prospect of being allowed to go and fight in a war?

We were marched from Redhill to Guildford a few days after registering our names. Soldiers were always marched all but very long distances in those days simply because there was hardly any traffic on the roads and that was what marching was for!

We caught the train, I remember, to Norwood and pitched camp there. If I remember correctly ten of us shared a tent and great armies of rats came round to visit us during the night. I wasn't used to this at all. I just couldn't believe it was happening!

Next day we discovered just how raw the army thought us as they began to try to sort us out into some kind of manageable group. I asked if I might join the flying corps. I knew there was no chance of being allowed to fly, but the flying corps was such a glamorous thing at the time that I wanted to be part of it and I thought I would have a good chance with my coachbuilding experience – all planes at that time were built of wood and canvas. I thought I would be useful but, unfortunately, they already had too many men. The service corps also had too many volunteers, so I was rather stuck and was beginning to wonder what on earth I would end up doing.

We stayed at Norwood while the Battle of the Somme was taking place. We were marched up and down every morning and taught how to turn right and left while doing so as if our lives depended on it. Then just as we'd really settled in we were moved to Northampton. In the market square there's an old coaching inn with a skating rink built behind it. That's where we were given yet more drill practice. And it was a rather funny sight to see virtually the whole of Northampton turn out each Sunday morning to see us march to church.

We were always amused by this church going because we were led in by our sergeant-major. He was one of the most outrageous swearers outside church but once through the doors he was a changed man. He sang all the hymns with what looked like real religious fervour and he knew all the responses.

We were eventually put into the King's Royal Rifles and then one day we were paraded in a nearby school playground. An end terrace-house overlooked the playground and on it was a big advertisement for Nestlé's milk. We were marched to a position so many yards from this advertisement and then a brigadier suddenly appeared from nowhere. He started at the end of the row of soldiers and moving along asked each man the same question: 'How good's your eyesight?' If you said it was good he asked you to read the words on the Nestlé advertisement. The ones who could read it were told to fall out on the right, the ones who could not went to the left. I could see the words clearly enough so I stepped to the right. But like the others I still had no idea what was going on. There were perhaps three or four hundred of us on the right and we were quickly marched off to the nearby barracks. Here a board had been fixed across at about head height. We had to stand under this and if our heads touched it we were accepted, although into what we didn't yet know. I was too high by half an inch. If you were 5 ft 8 in or less you joined the newly-formed tank regiment because you were an ideal height to fit inside the thing.

In spite of being turned down for the air corps, the service corps and now the tank corps I was eventually accepted in the machine-gun corps which, like the tank regiment, was just being formed at this time. So much was new – planes, rapid-fire guns, tanks and so on that the army was in a state of turmoil starting new regiments for this and that new invention.

We were sent to a huge camp near Grantham in Lincolnshire. Eight regiments were based there, each with its own mess room and guardroom and I believe more than forty thousand troops were trained there during the war.

We were taught how to be good infantry and, of course, we were taught to use the Vickers .303 machine-gun. This was also used as an anti-aircraft gun and we were taught the special skills of trying to bring down aeroplanes with it. We were issued with a special device to assist with aiming. This was a thing with two concentric circles that fitted on top of the gun. If you estimated that an enemy plane was, say, below 500 ft you aimed using the smaller circle. If it was above 500 ft you used the larger circle. And the system as I recall worked very well, although I have no idea why or how!

So, in between doing lots of marching and sentry duty, we learned to use the Vickers gun against men, aeroplanes and just about everything else. Vickers guns were manned by four men and I quickly became friends with my three fellow gunners. By this time it was 1916 and, having completed our training, we were ordered overseas.

I remember we waited at ease, stretched out along a small village railway station platform. We waited and waited and then the train arrived, but we didn't get on it. No one ever told you anything in the army until the last minute and this was obviously going to be no exception to that rule. A major came along to give the order to board and just at that moment a motorbike messenger screeched to a halt by the platform and handed him a note. Then it was about turn and we were all marched off back to the camp. We discovered later that the plan was to keep us in reserve to be sent to Ireland to control the increasing violence of the struggle for home rule. They apparently needed two or three battalions for Ireland and ours was to be one of them.

Two days later it was all change once again and we were sent to Folkestone and put on a boat to France. I never discovered why they changed their minds about sending us to Ireland but at last we were heading for the front. Our feelings I suppose were a mixture of apprehension and exhilaration. Every man had felt it was his duty to go to the front and now that was where we were headed.

We arrived in France and were taken to Etaples, the biggest camp for new arrivals. We were there for a week during which we were told regularly what to expect in the weeks and months that followed. But being told is no real preparation, particularly as the people doing the explaining were concerned primarily to keep our morale up.

The machine-gun corps, of which I was a part, was divided up. Every battalion was allocated two machine-guns and two gun teams. Until that time the infantrymen – non-specialists as it were – had had the guns. I went with my team and our gun to join a Black Watch Battalion.

Things began to move very quickly after that. So much so that I was never really afflicted by the intense boredom of day after day spent inactive in the trenches. We moved up towards Ypres where the fighting was particularly fierce, but for some reason my division was held in reserve. The first time I saw action came when the Germans effectively pushed us back after the Battle of the Somme. We'd made a big dent in their defences but they were coming back at us. Tens of thousands of our men were killed.

Still my division was held in reserve and then, when the fighting reached its peak and casualties were coming in endlessly through the mud and filth, we were ordered to advance exactly 1,000 yards. I've always chuckled at the precision of that order amid the bloody chaos of the battlefield. The message was sent to us via a Sopwith Pup – a tiny one-man aeroplane that seemed to be able to land virtually anywhere under any conditions. The pilot would land, run across with his message, hand it over and then dash back to the plane and take off again. If it was a really tight spot the message or the orders would be thrown out of the plane on a tiny parachute.

Having received our orders we began to go forward through a landscape so terrible that words cannot really describe it. Everything was destroyed, blackened and there were craters and mud and devastation everywhere. We were supposed to be part of the spearhead designed to push the Germans back to their line at Bullycourt.

We – by which I mean my gun team – were positioned a few hundred yards from Bullycourt on a railway line. Just down the line from where we stopped was the station itself. This was to be the site of the bloodiest battle I was ever involved in. The station was vital to the Germans because they needed it to bring up their supplies and ammunition. We were told that we would have to take the station whatever the level of resistance. My gun team and I supported the division when it went over the top to take the station. And such was the strategic importance of the place that the Germans sent up their élite Prussian Guard to defend it. Within twenty minutes of our men going over the top three-quarters were either dead or seriously wounded. They were cut down in great endless swathes; cut to ribbons or blown to pieces. So much so that the remaining men had to jump over or run around the piles of dead and dying. Our orders as a machine-gun team were to back up the men and cover them. The battle raged at different levels of intensity for two weeks. One night we would take the station and village and hold it for a few hours against ceaseless and ferocious counter-attack, then the next night the Germans would have retaken it and we would hammer them as hard as we could. So many died in those two weeks that when the fighting was over we could not go into the village because of the stench of decaying bodies. It was unspeakable. You could have walked from one side of the village to the other over the bodies of the dead without once touching the ground.

I survived those two weeks and I know I mowed down dozens of Germans. It was just a job and you didn't think that the heavy bullets of the .303 machine-gun were cutting men to ribbons –

but, let's face it, that's what the bullets used to do. They'd cut a man's leg off or tear a line across his body doing so much damage that he would bleed to death in seconds. It was terrible but what else could we do?

After that battle I went on to Passchendaele and the battle for the Menin Gate. By this stage of the war I think we soldiers knew that the Great War was not a war for heroes. We were not to be covered in glory by it and our officers knew we knew this. Thus when it came to the battle for the Menin Gate our major came to us, to the four in my machine-gun team, and said that in a couple of days he was going to ask us to do a very difficult thing, but that if we did it he would guarantee that we were given a break from the front line fighting. That 'difficult thing' turned out to be an order to take up a position in a trench just 20 yards from the German front line trench – a distance that was, in reality, nothing. Once we were in position we could hear the Germans talking. We could hear them even when they spoke fairly quietly and, of course, they must have known we were there. We were told we had to hold this position whatever happened.

It sounds like an almost suicidal thing to be asked to do, but in fact we were helped by our very closeness to the Germans. Had we been further away from their trench they could have shelled our position from way back behind their front line. But with only 20 yards separating us from their men it was too dangerous. We thought they would never risk shelling us in case they hit their own men.

Our trench was filthy and waist deep in thick, sodden mud, but we had to stay crouched all the time. If we'd stood up we would have been spotted and shot at by snipers immediately.

On the morning before the battle began our guns started the usual bombardment. We used 12 in naval guns and when a shell from one of these hit the ground the noise and destruction were incredible. One shell hit the corner of a concrete pillbox up ahead of us and instantly dozens of Germans rushed out of it scattering everywhere. We realized we were in trouble when a couple of German shells crashed close to our position. They'd got our range and that was it. It's odd though because although we knew we could neither move out of our trench nor stay in it without being killed we stayed pretty calm as I recall. I think this is largely because when something is inevitable you often accept it calmly. Minutes later we were hit. All I remember was a great whoosh and being thrown violently to one side. Then I blacked out. I'd been badly injured all down one side and I was bleeding from my arm and leg on my left side. But I was lucky I suppose. One of my friends was killed and the other two injured like me. The man who died obviously took the full force of the blast.

Injured and suffering badly from shock we were of no more use so we scrambled back from the front to the nearest casualty clearing station. I can remember almost nothing of this time. I suppose the shock effect of having been hit numbed me to everything and later on when I'd recovered that same shock prevented me from remembering the details.

Anyway when I reached the medical oficer he checked me over and said, 'I don't want to send you home but you can't stay here'. I was put on a stretcher and into an ambulance with three other injured men. I remember the journey seemed to take forever, but we eventually reached one of the field hospitals. It was run by Australian nurses and it was like being in heaven. It was so quiet and peaceful after the front.

Suddenly I was given wonderful food and drink – the kind of food and drink I hadn't had for months. I was in that field hospital for two or three days and then a nurse came along and said simply, 'You're going home to England.' I couldn't really believe it. I'd been expecting to be sent back to the front, but instead I was issued with special kit – a curious kind of woolly jersey, warm hat and so on – and sent off to a hospital ship at Rouen.

I can remember the swivel beds – they were on swivels to keep them level whatever the sea conditions – and the marvellous soup we were fed. I have never tasted anything like it before or since. The boat sailed for Southampton and the next thing I knew I was lying on a stretcher on Southampton station platform with a dozen other stretcher cases. We were put into a special hospital train which had huge windows and having assumed I was going home to Redhill I was more than a little surprised to discover that the train was going to Manchester. We were taken to Manchester's Lily Lane School which had been turned into a hospital. Everything to do with the military seemed to involve moving in those days because no sooner had we arrived than we were moved to Ashton-under-Lyne. I remember being taken into a new hospital here. It was right next to the workhouse pigsty!

Things didn't go well with my injuries. They weren't terribly serious but they weren't healing well so I was sent to convalesce for nine months at Ripon in Yorkshire. And I was still there when the Armistice was signed towards the end of 1918.

Of course, I was still in the army in spite of the fact that the war had ended, but there was an army law which said that any man who'd been in hospital was entitled to two weeks leave. The men in my ward knew this, but none of us was given any leave. We asked an officer and he just brushed the question aside. Next day our sergeant-major ordered us to fall in and we simply stayed on our beds. We were on strike! A dangerous thing really because, of course, in the army refusal to obey an order can lead to a court martial. The sergeant-major got a lieutenant to speak to us and still we refused to move. Next they tried a captain and then a major, but still we refused to take any notice. I can't think how we managed to be so brave now! In the end a brigadier was sent to talk to us and we stood to attention when he came into the ward. We explained the problem and he turned furiously to the major and asked if it was true that we had not been given our leave. Next thing we knew we had all been given our two weeks. That must be one of the few mutinies that actually worked and didn't get the participants into serious trouble!

I went home to Redhill and stupidly discovered that my leave ended on Christmas Eve. I must have still had the spirit of rebellion in me because I simply went AWOL. I wasn't going to go back on Christmas Eve. My father had been discharged and I hadn't seen him for a long time so I just wasn't having any of it. I had a lovely Christmas at home and then when I reported back I discovered that scores of men hadn't turned up at the right time. We were given two weeks fatigues as a punishment, but it wasn't really taken seriously. Having been given my punishment I set off back towards my hut but someone shouted across to me and said I was wanted in the guardroom. I knew at this time that trained men were being formed into an army of occupation and I thought well that's what they want me for. When I got to the guardroom the sergeant asked me a few questions about my injuries and my time in hospital. He looked me up in some files and suddenly turned round and said 'You lucky bugger! You're getting your discharge.' Almost every soldier thought he might get out in a year or so, but I was told I could leave at the end of the week. I couldn't believe it. When I got back to Redhill, an army man no more, my mother was working quietly in the garden. She got such a fright when she saw me.

It's such a long, long time ago now – more than seventy-five years – and almost everyone from that time has gone, but my dominant memories I suppose are of the machine-gun shaking in my hands as I pressed the triggers with my thumbs; of watching the enemy soldiers being hit by bullets that I had fired and of walking over the dead at Passchendaele. But I remember many details too. I remember at night seeing great armies of rats – literally hundreds of them – moving across the battlefield like a battalion. And I remember days spent in the routine of the trenches. It wasn't all death and destruction, unless you were involved in a battle. We might be on sentry duty or practising for another stunt, another battle. I remember that machine-gunners like us were hated by the infantry. I don't mean personally, but they knew that if they were near our position there was an increased chance that they would be hit because the Germans always tried to work out where the machine-guns were and then, of course, they shelled them.

Back in Redhill I returned to the coachbuilders for a time, but then decided to go to Manchester University to train as a congregational minister. I did my training and worked in the church from then on. I was naval chaplain to the men of HMS *Tormentor* during the second war, but that's another story. I enjoyed being a chaplain, but I don't really know if my experiences in the Great War led to my longing for the church. My war lasted about eight months – long enough, but at least I came home alive. In spite of my injuries I've been pretty healthy ever since. In fact I preached my last sermon – it was exactly fifteen minutes long – when I was ninety.

CHAPTER EIGHT

OLIVER 'ANDY' ANDREWS

Oliver 'Andy' Andrews was born in Deanshanger, South Buckinghamshire in 1897. His earliest memories are of a world remote from the big cities and towns, a world where the pattern of daily rural life had changed little in centuries. Andy grew up among the fields and lanes of an essentially pre-industrial part of England where the pace of life was determined almost entirely by the horse. Andy's father worked for a company that made harvesters and it was therefore a natural progression for Andy to leave school and go straight into farming.

Yes, I left school very early – I would have been thirteen or perhaps fourteen. Very few village lads stayed on much after that. And it was only a village school. We learned our catechism and how to read and write, but I was really only a boy when I left to go on the land.

I started as a lead boy with the horses. For ploughing and harrowing and so on that was all we had in those days, but there was something marvellous about working with a horse although, like everyone else, I didn't realize it until they'd all vanished and tractors had taken over. Apart from leading the horses I used to be the farm egg collector. When I'd collected enough eggs – I can't remember how many – I'd set off from Deanshanger to Stony

Stratford where I used to deliver them to the farmer who had the old mill. It was a round trip of about 12 miles and, of course, I had to walk. There was no other way to get there. No buses, of course, in a remote rural place like that and no one could spare a horse for half a day.

My strongest memory of those early days on the farm is of leading a horse that was pulling a ribbed roller up a field. When you were leading a horse doing this sort of work you walked behind it and at the side, but I was a lazy little so-and-so and I used to jump up on to the shafts to save walking. So if you imagine it I was right behind the horse sitting crossways on the shafts and with the roller just below and behind me. Well, one day we were moving quite happily up the field when I decided I'd had enough walking so I made a jump at the shafts, missed or tripped or something and fell over. Luckily I dropped into a furrow because next thing I knew the roller had gone over me. I wasn't hurt because the ground was soft and as I say I'd gone into a furrow. An old boy was ploughing with a team about a field away and he'd seen what happened. I heard him shout at me, 'Serves you bloody well right!' Just at that moment his ploughshare hit a flint or a stone and the handles came up and hit him hard under the chin. I took great delight in shouting back at him, 'Serves you right too!' He was in the right really though because to do the job properly I should have been walking quietly beside the horse.

After my time on the farm I got a job as a layer-on for the Whitefriars Press, part of the Bouverie Press empire. A layer-on fed the paper through the machinery and I was doing that when war broke out. Although we lived in what was a fairly remote part of the country the talk everywhere was of the war and all the other lads were off immediately to join up. That was the reason I went. It was as simple as wanting to be with my friends and we were all caught up in the excitement and adventure of it. No one really thought it was going to be a terrible business because we hadn't had any experience of a war close to home for so long. Anyway, when I joined up I had to lie about my age – I added a year to make sure I was able to join the happy band! So I was seventeen and said I was eighteen. They never queried it.

I actually took the King's shilling at Tunbridge in Kent where I'd gone with a group of lads from the Whitefriars Press. I joined the 7th Battalion, the West Kents and we were sent for intensive training – that's what I think they used to call it – at Salisbury. I seem to remember that we were inspected by a very bored looking King George at one stage.

After my training my first job – would you believe? – was with the coastguard at Yarmouth. We used to go up and down the coast between Lowestoft and Yarmouth in a boat keeping an eye out for German boats. I think there was an idea that the Germans would try to invade. Anyway they didn't and I don't think we spotted a single suspicious boat.

Eventually I was sent to France. I think I probably went in the end because so many men were being killed and they were searching around for anyone able-bodied enough to go. My first memory is of marching through France across the fields and never on the roads. The idea was that we didn't want the Germans to hear us and I suppose it made sense because by this time we were quite close to the front. Having walked all night I remember we came to a halt in the middle of a corn field. We were exhausted so when we were told to stop we shouted and cheered. That was a big mistake because our commander immediately made us get up and march round the village twice. Having done this after marching all night and with a full pack, shovels and picks hanging off me, I got into my billet, flopped down and slept without removing anything.

It was a marvellous sleep, too, in spite of the fact that I was weighed down with all my army equipment. I'd probably been asleep for just a few minutes when I heard someone shout, 'Tea's up!' I rallied a bit at the sound of that and spotted a huge dixie full of tea so thick and strong that a teaspoon really would have stood up in it.

Soon after this I was sent to place called Albert on the Somme and it may seem hard to believe but I still thought it was all a game, a bit of a lark. I just couldn't take it seriously. None us us young soldiers did, at least at this stage. I was only seventeen remember and you think you can do anything and everything when you're seventeen. As it was all a bit of fun I was really rather enjoying myself and I was never hungry – there were army biscuits all over the place that you could eat at any time, even though they were a bit like dog biscuits.

We went through the usual routine of six days in the trenches and then six in reserve and, of course, all the time men were being killed and injured. They'd get hit by stray shells or by sniper fire if they were unlucky and although we saw it all the time I don't think we ever got used to it. But there's a shock effect on the man himself who's hit so it's less terrifying for the others. A hit man tends to be quiet initially because of the shock and in most cases he's taken away by stretcher-bearers before too long so the rest of you don't have too much time to brood. And discipline helps. You have the support of all your mates and somehow that makes you feel that the last thing in the world you could do would be to let them down. And there's no doubt that, however shocking it is to see someone killed or badly injured in front of you and to realize that you might be next, you do somehow come to accept it. Perhaps one of the reasons for this in the Great War was that so many men really did want a blighty – in other words a wound that was bad enough to get them back to England but not so bad as to kill or permanently injure them.

We lived through the days and weeks of relieving men in the front line trenches and then ourselves being relieved, and each time you survived your six days in the front line you had a great feeling of elation and sometimes sadness if one or more of your friends had been killed or badly injured.

My company was put in the second line on the first day of the Somme, 1 July 1916. The second line is of course dangerous but it's not nearly so bad as the front line. We were being kept there to provide a defence should that prove necessary. On 1 July early in the morning our commanding officer told us to get our heads down — he meant we were to get into our dug-outs. These were just excavations in the side walls of the trenches, not the sophisticated bunkers we later discovered that the Germans had built for themselves down in their trenches.

From our dug-outs we could look up and back over the tops of the trenches towards our guns. And it was an incredible sight. There were French 75s jammed wheel to wheel, aiming over our heads at the German front line and when they all began to fire together the noise for us — just yards in front of them — was indescribable. Then we were given the order to advance and as we did so the barrage lifted and moved forward. We then began to go forward toward the German line. Of course the barrage hadn't helped one bit because as soon as we got closer to the German line they all leapt up out of their deep concrete dug-outs and blasted away at us with machine-guns.

I had what many people thought of as one of the worst jobs in the trenches — I was a runner. That meant that I had to take messages across the battlefield, sometimes right in the middle of a battle if our communications wire had been broken by German shelling and that happened all the time. I lasted for quite a few months as a runner before I was wounded — much longer than the average I think, but eventually the day came. It was during the Battle of the Somme and I had to go from our part of the line to see if the Queen's Regiment was in contact with us. I remember I was given my order to take a message soon after we started our advance.

We'd come out of our trench and immediately met fierce fire from shells and heavy machine-guns — so much so that our men were very quickly bogged down in shell holes. The German machine-guns and shelling were so ferocious that we could neither go forward nor back and my commanding officer decided he wanted to find out if the line was unbroken between us and the next lot. It was a particularly dangerous thing to have to do, I suppose, because we were under such heavy fire and I can remember diving in and out of shell holes as I made my way through the smoke and chaos across the battlefield. Though I didn't have much time to think about it, I can also remember stepping over the bodies of my comrades. That's the memory that has really stayed with me from that time. It was terrible, but I had no choice but to go on.

I'd gone some way – I couldn't possibly tell you how far – and was constantly looking back to get my bearings for the return journey. It was so easy to get lost in that uniformly devastated landscape. I reckon I'd got about half way – it's difficult to be exact because shells were blowing the ground and bits of men into the air all around me and I really hardly knew where I was. Then, as I turned my head back to make a check of the ground I'd already covered, I felt a sort of stinging slap in the face. I think the sniper must have been hiding up the remains of a nearby tree. I can't remember now why I thought that but it was definitely the idea that flashed into my mind at the time. I knew I'd been hit but I wasn't quite sure whether it wasn't just a scrap of something that had perhaps only scratched me. It was only later that I realized a sniper's bullet had hit me in the face. The bullet went in through one cheek and came out the other and, almost at the same moment, a shell burst nearby and a piece of shrapnel caught me higher up on my head. I was knocked senseless for a moment and the bullet didn't do my teeth a lot of good, but even in my stunned state I was able to stagger back across the shell holes and mud in what I thought must be the direction of the British trenches.

Next minute I stumbled into a trench and came across a German! He beckoned me to stay with him but I wouldn't. I pressed my hands to my bleeding face, one on either side, got back out of the trench and eventually reached a Red Cross station. To be honest I only remember vaguely how I got there. I was in shock and staggering around amid the confusion of the battle so I think finding the medicos was more luck than judgement. Anyway, someone at the Red Cross station took one look at me and told me to keep going until I reached a casualty clearing station.

Here I was put on a stretcher and into an ambulance. By this time it was dark, but all around were the distant booms and flashes from shells as we bumped our way slowly away from the front line. I was horrified as I lay in the ambulance to discover that my clothes were soaked with blood. I thought I'd had it and must be very badly wounded, but I don't remember feeling much pain.

I spoke to another man who lay near me and asked if he would ask the driver to stop. I think I thought the bumping and rocking would finish me off and I was beginning to feel terrible. The driver shouted back that he could see lights ahead and that we should hang on. Eventually I remember we swerved into the grounds of a hospital at Le Touquet. There were attendants everywhere and they got me out in a flash. Next thing I knew I was in a hospital bed – the first bed I'd been in for months. I'd been in France for more than a year and I know that as a runner I was very lucky to survive the war at all.

I didn't get to look at my face until I was on the hospital train. I was given a top bunk and I can remember rolling off the bed and crawling along the corridor to the loo where I saw two of the worst black eyes you can imagine and two great pads stuck to my cheeks. I couldn't believe it was me, but I'm afraid it was. I was asked where I lived and assumed that the authorities would send me to a hospital somewhere near my home, but they did the exact opposite. They sent me as far away as they could. I think they thought I would be dispirited if too many of my friends and relatives came to see me and they didn't want that for the simple reason that they wanted me back at the front as soon as I was ready again. Anyway, I went to Cardiff for a while. I was looked after very well, but it's always seemed rather sad to me that they sent me there because, as I explained to one of the nurses, there was no way my mother could afford to come to visit me.

I was back at the front by early 1917, along with a number of other wounded men who'd recovered sufficiently to be sent back. When our colonel saw us he said, 'Who sent you poor buggers back?' The sergeant-major was a little kinder. When he heard that I'd been shot through the face he ordered that I was to be fed minced meals which I thought was rather decent of him. I never returned to the front line, but was sent instead to the labour corps well back from the front. From there I was eventually sent to Ireland and then, in 1918, discharged as unfit for further service. In total I'd done four years and sixty-three days. I'd joined four months after the war started and I was discharged four months before it ended. I was given two blue wound stripes.

Back in England I worked for a printing firm for a while and then with the £400 I was offered instead of a pension I bought a pony and cob – a sort of little trailer and I set up a round in the Bedford area delivering fruit, vegetables and other bits and pieces. My dad was very rude about the pony – he always used to say it was religious because it was always going down on its knees! I don't know about that, but he certainly used to go to sleep every time I stopped to make a delivery. After that I worked for the Civil Service for many years. I came to Deeping St James here in Lincolnshire in 1952 and I've been here ever since.

I suppose the most remarkable thing about my experience in the Great War is that a man who joined up with me all those years ago is still alive and we've kept in regular touch all that time. I suppose that says something about how the war brought people together.

CHAPTER NINE

TOM BROACH

Tom Broach was born in Singapore in 1898. His father, an army schoolmaster, spent his working life moving around the world teaching the children of officers and men. The family moved every two or three years and from Singapore, when Tom was only three, they moved to India. This was still in the great days of the Raj and Queen Victoria was, of course, still Empress of India. Having safely given birth to three children Tom's mother died as a result of her next confinement. Now ninety-three, he recalls these events of long ago with a calm resignation borne of a life that he admits himself was narrowly cheated from death. Tom came, on his mother's side, from a long line of Devon farmers, so when he returned from India in 1910 at the age of twelve and his father was posted to Aldershot, the young Tom was sent away to his grandfather's farm near Devonport.

There were no jobs to be had and no dole so I had to do something and I rather liked the idea of learning to farm dairy cattle. I'd always liked living in the countryside – I still do – so it seemed like a good idea. I'd been working with grandfather for five or six years when I received my call-up papers. Like everyone of my age or thereabouts I'd expected to get them, but it was still a bit of a shock when they arrived. I was nearly eighteen when I set off for the Exeter depot. About one hundred youngsters from that part of Devon were gathered there when I arrived and we were sent to Chiseleton Camp near Swindon I remember. I spent six terrible months here – it wasn't as bad as being at the front by a long way, but it was my most terrible experience at the time. I couldn't believe it and I still don't quite know how I survived. The winter of 1916 was absolutely terrible and we had to sleep in tiny bell tents, one man to a seam as they used to say.

We were trained very intensively; how to use our rifles, marching, and masses of bayonet practice. We also learned how to dig in – in other words how to dig a trench big enough for one man. We were shown how to cover ourselves with a groundsheet once we'd dug the hole. It was difficult to see the point of it all but we were told to do it so we did it. We were constantly charging sandbags and being told where and when to fix our bayonets. From Chiseleton I was sent on to Broadstairs in Kent from where, just after Christmas 1917, I was at last sent to France. It all seemed a bit of an adventure at that stage because we didn't really know what to expect. The newspapers had no real reports about what was going on and there was no television or radio. We were scared of course – no, apprehensive, is probably a better word.

Our first stop in France was Rouen where so many British troops got their first taste of life in France. Here the hundred or so from my batch were divided into two lots – fifty went to the First Hampshire Regiment and fifty to the Dorsets. When the experienced soldiers first laid eyes on us they were very rude. I heard a couple shout at us, 'Good god, why have they sent us you little bastards?' But within a few days we had our first taste of the trenches because we were sent to the front line to relieve the Grenadier Guards at Arras.

The first thing we were told – and it was repeated again and again to get it into our heads – was at all times keep your head down. When you first arrive in a trench it's easy to think the dangers are being exaggerated, but in many cases the least peep over the top (great temptation to a new arrival) would mean a bullet whistling past your ear or instant death. We quickly discovered that the Germans had snipers watching for the least sign of the top of a head.

The trenches at Arras were relatively good ones – they were very deep so you could move around without too much danger from sniper fire. Each day at dawn we would stand to on the raised board at the front of the trench and I always imagined the line of men standing a few yards apart for hundreds of miles along those twisting turning, seemingly endless trenches.

Once the stand to was over a detail would set off to collect our rations – some tea and bread and jam. We used to heat the water for our tea with great difficulty, but the trick was to get a candle, break it into three short pieces, tie the three pieces side by side using a bit of old webbing and then light all three pieces of candle at the same time. A bully beef can filled with water and held above the flames from the three candles would boil in a few minutes. We used to hold the can above the flames using our bayonets. I don't know what the army would have made of that officially, but we used to do it. And luckily there was always plenty of tea. We always got a cigarette ration, too, and some chocolate, but as I didn't smoke I used to swap my cigarettes for chocolate.

After breakfast we'd be organized into working parties to do lots of different jobs – we might be filling sandbags or repairing stretches of the trench. We were always pretty busy and I don't remember being bored. The problem was that now and then, perhaps once a week or once a fortnight someone would let off a shot from either side and all hell would break loose for a while, with shelling and rifle fire and so on. Then just as quickly it might all die down again.

For each company in a trench there were always two companies held in reserve so we would spend six days in the front line trench, followed by six in what you might call a second line trench. Then after twelve days we'd be sent back about 2 miles from the front to be de-loused and to rest of course. After two weeks in either the front line or the back-up trench we were filthy and heavily infested so on each and every occasion that we went back we had to go through the de-lousing procedure. At first it seemed dreadful to be so badly infested with lice but after a while you got used to it. You had to, because it was unavoidable.

At the de-lousing station we would strip completely naked and throw our clothes into an incinerator – it wasn't really an incinerator because you got your clothes back but they were given some kind of high temperature treatment I think to kill all the bugs. In the meantime we'd be pushed into a kind of portable shower. This was in a shed and once you were in you were simply doused with a hell of a lot of water. At first it was freezing, then it would warm up a bit, and then it would nearly scald you.

Once out of the showers we'd rush to grab our clothes as they were thrown back at us – you often had to pick up and wear whatever was to hand. The worst part of the clothing was the puttees – these were continually soaked from the knee-deep water in the trenches. I suppose the men in my company were lucky, at Arras anyway, because for much of our stint there we were near a stream where at least we could wash our hands and faces regularly.

When we were away from the front we'd go down to the local village and have a drink and there were concert parties about once a week, so it wasn't all doom and gloom. After six days of this comparative bliss we were sent back to the trenches. If you worked it out month by month we spent twenty-four days in the trenches for every twelve days spent out of them.

What everyone dreaded more than anything – and it was always at the back of your mind – was going over the top. The phrase has become part of the language now, but if you can imagine we were told not even to peep over the top of the trench ever, and then to know that one day we would have to expose ourselves completely to the enemy who was just sitting there waiting for us to show so he could simply pick us off. We had been given some training in what to do when the time came to go over – we were told to fix our bayonets to the tops of our rifles but not to fire unless we had a distinct target.

I remember having to go over the top at a place called La Basse. It was early in 1918. I remember we'd dug some new trenches near a canal and the Germans – unfortunately for us – used this canal as an aiming point. That was why we had to move forward. We were just told to go forward and we had to do it. It was soon after the big offensive from Arras of 21 March 1918. We'd push the Germans back, but then, inevitably, they'd counter-attack and force us back. It was always like that. We'd push them and then they'd push us. Lots of our trenches were overrun during their counter-attack and we lost a lot of men, killed and injured or taken prisoner. It was a huge nightmare of a battle.

But I remember that when we went over the top things had changed since the early days of the war. Early on when the soldiers got up out of the trenches and moved towards the enemy they'd line out and walk with their rifles held aslant and, of course, they were easy targets, particularly as they were taught to go steadily forward without running or dodging and weaving. It was absolute madness, but then the generals who were well back from the line always thought that the barrages that took place before an advance would knock out the enemy. When this didn't happen and our men started to be mown down in their thousands it was too late to change tack. But later in the war, by the time my lot went over, we did it in single file – that way we were much less of a target. And we went in waves. One batch of men would go, there would be a pause and then off would go another. Subsequent waves had to run across or around the bodies of hundreds of the dead and injured.

We moved forward, running, crouching and dodging, not that it did much good as there were shells pitching all around and it was entirely a matter of luck whether or not you were hit. It was very confusing, too, with the terrific whizzing of incoming shells and shrapnel and the explosions all around as they came down. You never stopped to help those who were hit. Never. That may seem terrible but there was no point. Hopefully they would be gathered up later by the stretcher-bearers. You just kept going till you were hit or you reached your objective. When you went over you were always given an exact objective. At Arras our officers told us to aim for the corner of a distant wood – it would have been about 1,000 yards from our front line trench. We were told to get there, dig in and at all costs stay there. I remember that just before we started out I was shaking all over with fear. We all were I think, but somehow I reached the edge of the wood without being hit. I don't know how and I remember little about it except stumbling and running through the smoke and the noise and the soil thrown up by exploding shells.

When we arrived at the edge of the wood we split into pairs and one man began digging in while the other kept firing to keep him covered. My partner did the digging while I kept up the firing, but all the time rifle bullets would be throwing up soil all around us. When you're under that kind of fire it's amazing how fast you can dig. Several of my friends were killed instantly here, but men were always being killed and often when they thought they were fairly safe.

I remember one chap was killed before he got into his first trench. As soon as you got near the front line trenches you would often be under fire and shells would be coming down all the time. This young man was killed instantly on the way in. A shell just happened to land next to him and he was blown to nothing. Some men were torn to pieces, others just looked like dolls that had been discarded.

We lost a lot of men and officers during that offensive at Arras. Once you were out in an exposed position you had the additional dangers of getting your rations and supplies. These were sent up at night but it was still very dangerous with unexploded shells everywhere and snipers and flares. Our bread, cheese and onions I remember would arrive in a sandbag and five men shared the provisions contained in each sandbag. These included chocolate and cigarettes too, so it was all mushed up together! During the

Germans' massive counter-attack at Arras they even managed to capture our rations! We weren't too happy about that I can tell you.

One thing people often forget is that in many cases the British front line trench might be only 50 yards from the German front line trench. In other areas it might be 200 to 300 yards across no man's land. In the ordinary run of events – unless a battle was raging, for example – we were told not to fire unless there was a very good reason. That was because if you took a pot shot at something it would be likely to bring the roof down and the other side would go mad for a few minutes firing with everything they'd got – panic stations as we used to call it. You could always be sure that if you fired they would fire back.

Sometimes all would be quiet for a long time and then there would be general hell for two or perhaps three hours. I dreaded the night most because you would see ghostly shapes moving quickly and you never knew when they might attack. Fighting at night is particularly terrifying because you're disorientated by the darkness and the whole thing is a nightmare of confusion and panic. Sometimes at night we'd be sent out to a shell hole – you creep out half running then dive into it – to listen to our bayonets. By that I mean we'd stick the bayonet in the ground and then listen to it – the idea was to try to discover if the Germans were tunnelling.

In winter the trenches were indescribably terrible. To get up out of the mud we'd dig tiny holes just big enough to sit in along the sides of the trench walls and then we'd use a groundsheet to keep the rain and draughts out.

I have nothing but admiration for our officers – they were so helpful and considerate. And although a lot more rank and file were killed, proportionately a lot more officers were killed and seriously wounded.

My war continued at Cambrai where month after month the battle raged. The Germans took it, we took it back, they attacked again and so on, seemingly endlessly. It was after the relief of Cambrai that I was wounded. I was a corporal, acting medical sergeant at the time. I'd taken two men to a first-aid post at Haspre I remember and I was in a slit trench about 6 ft long. Suddenly there was a bang! I'd heard the whizz of the shell as it passed over and then a terrific bang as it hit the ground. I was blown into an officer and sergeant-major who'd been talking to each other just in front of me. I can remember the searing pain and being treated by a doctor who soaked a big piece of cotton wool in iodine and pushed it right inside the wounds in my side. The pain was incredible, but from the moment I was hit to the moment I reached the casualty clearing station I never lost consciousness. It is a terrible thing to admit but the first thought I had was, 'I've got a blighty!' I suspect many of the soldiers were envious – I know they were. We all talked about getting a blighty – a wound or an injury just bad enough to get us back home and out of the war. And now I had mine. So instead of worrying about the injury I just felt relief. I thought, 'At last I'm going to get out of this and go home.' An ambulance picked me up to take me to one of the casualty clearing stations, but they were all full. There were several of us in the ambulance and the driver kept apologizing and telling us that we'd have to go on to the next station because the one he'd just tried was full. He was very apologetic and kept telling us not to worry. The casualty clearing stations were big marquees about 1 mile apart and stretching all along the front for mile after weary mile.

When I did get into one a doctor examined me and said I was going to be all right. I was operated on under anaesthetic and kept there for ten days. I remember that, like all injured men, I was given what we called a dolly bag – a cotton drawstring bag about 10 in square – and into this were placed all my personal effects. My regimental cap badge, my identification tags and my periscope – a little folding tin mirror we were all given to fit to the bayonet on our rifles so that we could look over the top of a trench without the risk of being hit by a sniper. These few items were put into this little bag and I still have the bag and its contents to this day. The ID tag had two discs, one reddish brown, the other green. If you were killed they left the khaki tag on you and sent the red one to the authorities who would inform the next of kin. My two tags are tied together on their original bit of string to this day.

Eventually I was sent to Boulogne where I waited two weeks for a hospital ship to take me back to England. My next stop was the Dudley Road Hospital in Birmingham. All the time I travelled back across England my main thought was, 'Thank god I'm out of that.' I suppose it was a reaction to what all the men felt in the trenches.

Looking back now it all seems unreal, but I can remember the general atmosphere of waiting nervously all the time for something to happen. There would be long lulls in the shelling and then the Germans would begin to suspect that we were up to something and they'd start shelling again. If you were in a trench and you saw something happening over toward the enemy, or if you saw someone moving out in no man's land you didn't fire, but passed the message along to the next soldier who passed it along in turn. In my eleven months in the trenches I don't think we either gained or lost a foot of land.

My very worst memory is undoubtedly of the massive bombardment of 21 March 1918. It started at 3 a.m. Both the Germans and the British used a creeping bombardment technique – shells were aimed to rain down at a certain range and that range was then gradually increased and the shells exploded further and further forward, killing and maiming as they went. After the bombardment or during it you'd suddenly see enemy soldiers running toward you and that's when you started to fire because you had at all costs to stop them getting to your trench.

One very useful weapon we had was the Mills bomb and during a battle you'd often hear someone shout, 'Give him a Mills!' meaning throw one of these things. It was a sort of pear-shaped hand grenade. You pulled out the pin and then threw it – you had four seconds once you'd pulled the pin before the thing exploded.

One very bad memory for me was being sent out into no man's land at night to bury one of my comrades. My sergeant-major simply said, 'Broach, out you go and bury Private James.' I said I didn't know what to do – this happened during my first week – and the sergeant was quite patient. He explained, 'Drag the body into the nearest shell hole and just cover it up with soil as best you can.' We had a stock of simple wooden crosses and I was given one of these to take out with me. I buried him out there alone in the dark and I can tell you I was terrified. Scared stiff the whole time. I was afraid that a Verey light – a flare – would go up. If you were digging and one of these things burst in the sky above you the worst thing was to dive for cover. The enemy would spot you moving in an instant so you had to keep stock still even though your automatic reaction was to take cover. Just imagine you're standing there totally illuminated and forbidden to move. You feel like an enormous target and you expect any minute to be hit and killed. I managed to bury Private James and get back safely but that was a terrible night; a night I've never forgotten.

The only bit of entertainment we got in the trenches was, I suppose, the rats. That sounds funny, but if we were bored we'd stick a bit of bread on the end of our bayonets, lay the rifle out along the top of the trench and wait for a rat to arrive. That didn't take long because they were everywhere. When a rat started to nibble the bread we'd pull the trigger and shoot it. It was just something to do.

The mud was difficult to cope with. Many men got trench foot – their legs swelled up so badly that they'd scream at you not to come anywhere near them in case you touched their legs. That's how painful they were. It was a kind of gangrene, I think. We were given a special oil – I don't know exactly what it was but you rubbed it on your feet and it was supposed to stop trench foot. I don't think it was effective for everyone by any means.

A lot of people think it must have been difficult to sleep in the front line trenches with so much mud everywhere and the constant risk of injury or death. Well, I can tell you it wasn't difficult to sleep at all. Anyone who has been very, very tired will tell you that at a certain stage you will sleep absolutely anywhere under any conditions. One of the most dangerous things was being asked to carry a message back from the front line – HQ was about a mile back from the front and frankly you dreaded being chosen to carry a message because you would be lucky if you made it.

Back in Blighty I was quickly discharged from the army by the Aldershot medical board – I still have my discharge certificate dated 6 January 1919 which stated that I was no longer fit for military service owing to injuries to the abdomen and buttocks. My injuries were pretty bad and it took a long time to recover from them. My wife thinks I've lived so long because of an inherited strong family constitution. That must be right I suppose. My dad was so disgusted at my invalidity pension – it was 8s. 8d. a week – that he appealed on my behalf and it was raised to 13s. It has been reviewed many times since then, but I still receive it every week.

After the war I went back to the dairy business. I was lucky to have a job because thousands of soldiers came back from the war and they were left penniless by the government. They sold matches in the street, washed dishes or starved. There was no dole in those days. I worked at the dairy business until we were bombed out of Devonport by Hitler in 1942. I went back to the farm after that and then retired finally in 1959.

I went back to Arras and the other places at which I'd fought in 1988, but I recognized nothing. Trees and grass have grown over everything and the trenches are gone, but in some places the ground is very lumpy and bumpy showing where the battles were fought. It was a strange and sad experience. I've tried to trace many of those who fought with me in the 1st Hampshires, but without success. I think they may all be dead now.

Some people say you came to accept death, but I don't think any of us really did. It affects you terribly when a man dies, but we had some happy times because there was such a sense of comradeship, which is something it is impossible to understand unless you have been part of it. We would all have done anything and everything to help another man.

CHAPTER TEN

BASIL FARRER

To judge by his handshake and fierce, independent air you might be forgiven for thinking that Basil Farrer is still in his late sixties or, at most, early seventies. In fact he is ninety-six and, incredibly, still smoking cigarettes and lambasting those who perpetuate what he sees as myths about the Great War. In many ways his experience of that conflict has a particular poignancy because for most of his active service he had what was probably the most dangerous job in the front line. He was a stretcher-bearer and to become one he'd had to move from a non-combatant unit to a front line unit. Basil Farrer was born in Manchester but quickly moved to Bradford in Yorkshire. He left school as soon as he was able and went straight into the Army. But, as he explained when I met him in his flat in Nottingham, his reasons for joining up were not exactly orthodox.*

I joined the army because a friend asked me to. It was as simple as that. The chap in question, whose name was Ernest, lived next door to us in Bradford with his father and older sister who did all the housework, the mother having died. Ernest was always having rows with this sister and he had to get away from her, or so he said.

Ernest and I usually met in the evenings, and we'd go for walks, often to Little Horton Park where there were swings, parallel bars

and rings on which we could exercise as if we were in a
gymnasium. Things came to a head one day and when I met Ernest
as usual, the first thing he did was to ask me if I would join the
army with him. I thought well, why not, it might be an adventure.
So, the next morning, 10 May 1913, we met as arranged and went
along to Bradford Moor Barracks which, at the time, was
unoccupied by troops except for a skeleton staff and a recruiting
sergeant whose post was at the barrack gate. Ernest was three years
older than I and, therefore, old enough to enlist, but I was well
below the required age. I was born on 31 August 1897, so on 10
May 1913 I was only fifteen. No one checked up on your age in
those days. All you had to do was pass the medical, which I did
quite easily after all the exercises I'd done on the bars and rings in
the park at home. I told the recruiting sergeant that I was eighteen
and that I would be nineteen the following January. I told him
2 January to be precise. This was a lie, of course, but although I
didn't know it at the time I'd picked my own saint's day. We
traditionally remember St Basil on 2 January.

Anyway, Ernest and I enlisted in the 3rd (special reserve)
Battalion, Alexandra Princess of Wales Own Yorkshire Regiment,
now officially known as the Green Howards. The terms of service
were six years, of which the first six months were spent in training
at the Depot, Richmond, Yorkshire. On completion of training the
idea was that one would return to civilian life and then be called up
annually for a training period of two weeks. We would also be
subject to immediate call-up in an emergency.

By the time we'd completed our six months training, my friend
Ernest had decided he didn't like the army life at all so he bought
himself out for £20. I was rather enjoying the whole thing, even
though most of our training consisted of drilling, manoeuvres and
bayonet practice, so I applied to enlist in the Regular Army, but
with a request that I be transferred to the Army Service Corps. I
can still remember the regimental sergeant-major at the depot
saying to me, 'Well, if you must leave us, join the Royal Army

Medical Corps – that way you'll at least have a chance of dying with your boots on.' Given that this was 1913 he clearly had a sense of what was soon to come.

The private soldier was paid a shilling a day then and all he had to know how to do was to keep fit and shoot well. Every year there was a shooting competition and you had to take part. If you were good and classified as a first-class shot you'd get 6d. on top of your wages; a second-class shot got an extra 4d.

In those days soldiers also had to sit written exams. We were sent to military school where we studied for one of three certificates. Passing with a third certificate didn't mean much, but with a second, a little harder to pass, you might become a sergeant; with a first you could eventually get into the commissioned ranks as a quartermaster.

I was quite a good shot, but I wanted to be on the administrative side so, as I say, I ended up in the Royal Medical Corps. I was posted to a hospital at Woolwich where I was trained pretty much as I suppose a St John's ambulanceman is trained today. We had to know about the structure of the body, its functions and so on.

I became a clerk and some time later, war having been declared in the meantime, I sailed for France. It was 14 August 1914, and I didn't know then that I was to spend my seventeenth, eighteenth and nineteenth birthdays fighting in Europe, before becoming a casualty on the Somme in mid-October 1916, six weeks after my nineteenth birthday.

All I can remember about my feelings when we set off for the front is that, like every soldier, I was young and very keen. It never really occurred to me that I might get killed or badly injured at that stage. But my next few birthdays were to pass almost unnoticed, at least by me.

We arrived at Boulogne on the Friday evening and disembarked the following morning. I recall seeing a French soldier on the quayside. With his blue greatcoat and red trousers, cigarette in mouth and rifle slung over his shoulder he reminded me of a poster advertising a play called *The Chocolate Soldier,* which was then showing in London.

To the cheers of the assembled population of Boulogne we marched up to a site overlooking the town and from there we could see the English coastline. There was a commemorative column which told us that we were at the place where Napoleon's Army had camped in preparation for the invasion of England. We were, I think, among the very first soldiers to arrive in France

After our night at Napoleon's camp, we were formed up on parade in the morning – it was a Sunday – and the Riot Act was read out to us by our commanding officer. We were read that part of the King's Regulations which deals with misdemeanours and the punishments to which a soldier was liable should he commit any of these misdemeanours while on active service. There was quite a list and the punishment for every offence was death. There were no two ways about it and we'd been warned so we couldn't plead ignorance later on.

That evening we entrained and arrived the following morning at Amiens where we were to set up a hospital. On Tuesday 18 August I sent home a field postcard – my first. On a field postcard you couldn't write anything at all. Instead you just crossed out the messages that didn't apply. I crossed everything out except the line which said 'I am quite well.' I still have the card, which is postmarked 18 August 1914, and it is unique in that it bears the embossed English postage stamp. These appeared only on the early issues. I was paid on that same day and I don't think there can be many soldiers left in England now who were paid in solid gold as I was then.

I have no clear memory of events during the week we remained in Amiens, but the Battle of Mons had been fought on 23 August and the big retreat had started. We left Amiens by train for Rouen where we remained in the railway station for the rest of the day, the main distraction being the frequent passage of trains full of American tourists desperate to leave the country on the first boat back to the USA.

Eventually we boarded a train for Le Havre where we stayed a day or two and then embarked on a ship that took us down the Channel, round the continental peninsula to unload us at St Nazaire. From there we entrained to travel eastward, our destination being the railway sidings at Villeneuve St George just south of Paris. If I remember rightly, we could just see the Eiffel Tower in the far distance.

Here, in the railway sidings, ambulance trains were being formed from *wagon-lits* passenger trains and I found myself posted to No. 5 ambulance train; we were a mixed crew made up of a French *médecin-major* (medical officer), two French orderlies, and our own medical officer with two or perhaps three RAMC orderlies. The Battle of the Marne was then in progress and we set off in that direction to reach the rail-head at Braisne where we were to take on the wounded. It was at Braisne that I first came under fire – the Germans were sending over high explosives which we called Jack Johnsons. Our train wasn't hit and when it had taken on its full capacity of wounded, we would return all the way back to St Nazaire, unload, and repeat the operation; the journey in both directions taking the best part of a week. This went on throughout the month of September and then, in October, we were sent north into Belgium.

The first Battle of Ypres was imminent, but the town itself was still full of civilians and the famous cloth hall still intact. Wounded were arriving at Ypres and it was here that I came across a chap I thought I knew. He was brought in badly wounded in the head, his eyes covered by a bandage, but he recognized my voice. By an extraordinary coincidence we had been together twelve months earlier at Richmond in Yorkshire. I only realized this when he suddenly said, 'I thought you'd left us, Farrer.' I told him I'd joined the Royal Army Medical Corps, but it was this encounter more than anything that made me decide to try to get a transfer to an active service unit at the front. In some indefinable way, meeting him changed my whole view of life. Ypres was a terrible battle and seeing the wounded brought in every day affected me greatly. The British Expeditionary Force was severely depleted but they saved the Channel ports and the Germans never took Ypres, although of course we held them at great cost in terms of lives lost.

As the Battle of Ypres drew to a close and the troops, on either side, settled down for the winter campaign, I was taken off the ambulance train and posted to a base hospital on the quayside at Boulogne. Then, some time early in 1915, I applied to be sent to the front and as a direct result of this application I was posted to No. 13 field ambulance, 13 Brigade, 5th Division. In spite of my experiences with the wounded and dying I was still just an enthusiastic kid — I was, after all, just seventeen. Anyway, with No. 13 field ambulance I soon found myself back in the Ypres sector. Our dug-outs were in the vicinity of what was called Hell Fire Corner and we had to cross this extremely dangerous area each time we needed to reach the regimental aid post to collect the wounded.

The division eventually left the Ypres Salient during the summer of 1915 to take over a part of the line then held by the French. This part of the line was on the Somme and we relieved the French 7th Division in trenches in front of what remained of a hamlet called Carnoy. I discovered later that the French top command had asked the British to extend their line, to take responsibility for more of it, which is why we were sent to the Somme, although I should emphasize at this point that ordinary soldiers like me were simply sent here and there without explanation and often as a result we hadn't a clue where we were. It was only after the war was over that soldiers gained a sense of their part in the overall scheme of things.

Anyway, one incident sticks in my mind from our first days on the Somme. On the morning following our takeover from the French, our troops found a live cow in a derelict farm building within rifle shot of the enemy. I did not actually see the animal or learn what became of it, but years later, in the early 1920s, I was talking to a French friend in Paris and mentioned the time when

I'd arrived in the French trenches in front of Carnoy. Without my having mentioned the incident with the cow, my friend asked what we had done with it! It transpired that the regiment in which my friend had been an officer had kept that cow there to provide fresh milk for the officers' mess. We'd relieved them during the night so they'd been unable to take the cow with them.

I wasn't too happy with my new place in the army so I applied yet again to be transferred – this time back to my old regiment, the Yorks. The request was granted and, in late 1915, I was sent back to base camp at Harfleur, near Le Havre. I was kitted out as an infantryman and, within a few days, posted to the 2nd Battalion, the Yorkshire Regiment. I quickly discovered that I was going to be back in the same area I'd recently quitted, in trenches in front of Carnoy. It was a time when the first units of Kitchener's New Army were arriving in France and two regiments, the 2nd Yorks and 2nd Wilts, were taken out of the 7th Division, but retaining their brigade number. They were joined by two of the new army, the Liverpool Pals, who paired up with the Yorks, and the Manchester Pals who paired up with the 2nd Wilts. They did turn and turn about in the trenches – six days in the front line and six days in reserve.

I very soon learned that in getting myself transferred back to my original regiment I'd actually jumped out of the frying pan into the fire. I think my application may have caused a bit of a stir in the officers' mess because it wasn't every day that a man voluntarily transferred from a non-combatant corps to the front line infantry and conscription had not yet been introduced in Britain, although all the other countries involved had long had it.

I was sent for by the medical officer attached to the regiment and questioned closely about my reasons for volunteering. 'So you're spoiling for a fight are you?' he said. I said I supposed I was and he replied, 'Well, I've just lost a stretcher-bearer and as you've been in the RAMC, you can take over.' I suppose I was a natural replacement, so that's what happened – I became a company stretcher-bearer. This was generally reckoned to be one of the worst jobs because you were in the open all the time and you couldn't get your head down and dig in, however fierce the battle. Regimental stretcher-bearers, originally bandsmen, remained infantrymen and did not wear a Red Cross arm band; they also remained legitimate targets for the enemy. Their duty was simply to collect the wounded as they fell and carry them to the regimental aid post from whence they were collected by the RAMC bearers. You have to remember, too, that as a stretcher-bearer you couldn't shoot back because you didn't carry a rifle and you had to stay in the open to help wounded men; you couldn't dive for cover into the nearest shell hole.

From January to 1 July 1916 our sector of the Somme was moderately quiet. There were, of course, continual casualties caused by shelling, sniper fire and raids – the latter a form of exercise insisted upon by our brass hats (who were themselves based way back to the rear) to maintain the soldiers' fighting spirit. Most nights listening patrols were sent out into no man's land, the idea being to try to find out what Jerry might be up to. But as the Germans followed a similar pattern, a meeting between a British listening party and a German one in no man's land was always a possibility and that, of course, could be very nasty.

During one of my early spells in the front line, B Company sent out a listening patrol which, unfortunately, got caught in the glare of a star shell (a Verey light) which illuminated the whole area. The result was that the listening party was machine-gunned. Two men succeeded in getting back safely to our lines, but not the corporal; when questioned, the two men who'd got back said they'd heard the corporal cry out, but thought he was telling them to get back.

After waiting for some time to see if the corporal would return we were convinced he must have been hit and word was passed down the trench for stretcher-bearers. My mate and I – stretcher-bearers, obviously, always worked in pairs – asked the men if they could give us some idea of their position when the machine-gun opened fire.

We then crawled out into no man's land with our stretcher. We had to move across the churned up slime and mud on our bellies and that wasn't easy because some of the shell holes were really quite deep and we had to cross barbed wire. It was the moaning of the corporal that drew us to him; when we found him we realized that he was very badly wounded in the stomach. I think he'd taken a full belt from the machine-gun right in his guts. Our arrival seemed to revive him, however, and he asked for a drink. It was part of our training not to give a man with a stomach wound either food or drink, so we told the corporal we'd get him back to our lines first. Then he started shouting and became delirious. Immediately the Germans heard the noise and up went the star shells accompanied by machine-gun fire in our direction. We had managed to drag ourselves and the wounded man into a shell hole that was just about deep enough to protect us from fire, but we were pinned down without any possibility of movement and I can recall thinking that if we didn't get away from there before dawn broke we were dead men. But we were lucky and soon the Verey lights stopped going up and darkness set in again. The firing had ceased when I heard the death rattle of the poor corporal. We placed him on the stretcher and started to drag it along the ground. We had to do it this way in spite of the weight of the body and the difficulty of dragging the stretcher through the mud and around all the shell holes because any attempt to stand up would have made us an easy target if a star shell went up. It was a very slow progress and all the time as we moved along I was sure I could hear slight noises behind us. I was sure we were being followed.

In spite of my suspicions we made it back to our line, but only just in time – two Germans who'd been following us had caught up just as we were lowering the corporal's body into our trench; our men spotted the Germans behind us and one chap literally reached over me, grabbed a German and hefted him into our trench. We didn't kill him because he might be able to tell us something useful. The second Jerry turned and made a run for it, but not before he'd managed to throw a hand grenade – what we called a spud masher – into our trench. We didn't know he'd done this till the next morning when we found the unexploded grenade in the mud at the bottom of the trench. Had that grenade gone off I would have been killed along with most of the others.

While returning with the corporal we'd had another close shave: we'd veered to the right as we approached our trench and were approaching the section held by A Company. Having heard the recent racket they were standing to on alert and when they saw us poor devils crawling towards them they were about to open fire. Just in time I managed to call out 'B Company stretcher-bearers coming in!'

I was lucky on that occasion and to a large extent it was luck that got me through the war, because I had a number of close shaves. I'll give you another example of how my luck always held.

During that January of 1916 the Yorks were in reserve, and my company, B Company, was billeted in a farm – Bamfray Farm, which was still occupied by the farmer and his family. We were rather lucky because the other companies were in a nearby wood, in tents. Bamfray Farm was situated a couple of kilometres behind the front line, some 100 yards down the road to Bray, after crossing the Albert–Peronne road. In January 1916 the farm was still intact, so we always considered it a fairly safe billet even though we were only in the cow shed. We felt so comfortable there that, contrary to orders, some of the fellows would more or less undress when settling down for the night. Strictly speaking you were always supposed to be fully dressed when in the front line or in one of the reserve areas. It was the Kaiser's birthday, I remember, sometime towards the end of January, and as a kind of birthday present our artillery had been beating the hell out of the German positions. There had been very little response to this from the German side, unless our Liverpool Pals in the front line were on the receiving end. Anyway, at the end of the day, we retired as usual when, bang, right in the middle of the night half-a-dozen shells came crashing down on the farm. We hopped it to the nearest dug-out and then someone called out 'Gas!'

With a feeling of horror I realized that in the rush to get into the dug-out I'd left my gas mask in the cow shed. What was I to do? I either exposed myself to the danger of being killed by shell blast or shrapnel in an attempt to retrieve my gas mask or I stayed put and risked death by phosgene. I decided that I'd better try to retrieve it. The entrance to the shed was in the middle of the side wall of the farm building, the animal stalls being on the right and left as one entered; I turned left just as a couple of shells fell shattering the right hand stalls. I quickly found my gas mask and returned safely to the dug-out. A close shave, but not surprising because, as I've said, you could be eliminated at any moment anywhere in the forward area. You simply had to accept the fact of death because you were confronted by it all the time; it was part of the daily routine from which there was no escape.

We were still holding that part of the line when, in June 1916, we were withdrawn to rehearse for the Big Push. We were sent to an area south of Amiens which was marked out with tape, supposedly to represent the German front line and with which we had to familiarize ourselves. Then, towards the end of the month we returned to the battle area, but behind the front line. For a full week, the last week of June, we listened to the ceaseless shelling of the German trenches by thousands of guns; it seemed impossible that anything or anyone could remain alive or in one piece after such a bombardment and we were assured that it was simply going to be a walkover.

We were in reserve, but I remember we had to go out on the night before the main attack to dig an advance trench. Basically this was just a shallow trench forward of our front line position. It was designed to get the men that bit further forward just before an attack. During the waiting period, I particularly remember that we were visited by a red-tabbed and red faced major. He gave us a talk on the proper use of the bayonet. It was ridiculous – talk about teaching your grandmother to suck eggs. During the night of 30 June we moved forward to take up our attacking positions. For B Company this meant a return to our old familiar section of trench in front of Carnoy, on the extreme right of the British line. We thought the bombardment was bound to have put paid to the German front line troops, but they'd built 30 ft dug-outs below their trenches compared to the pathetic dug-outs we had in the sides of our trenches.

On 1 July 1916 at precisely 7.30 a.m. our guns stopped firing, the officers' whistles sounded and we went over the top, our objective Montauban, just a few hundred yards away. Ours was one of just two objectives reached that day. We suffered bad casualties it's true, but amid scenes of some jubilation we captured our objective. I didn't realize it at the time, but we were incredibly lucky on our sector and casualties were low compared with those of the attacking troops on our left; but of the detailed events of the day I have scarcely any clear recall except for the deafening noise of bursting shells, the continual rattle of machine-gun fire and, at the end of the day, a feeling of great relief to be still alive.

Haig has been much criticized for what happened on the Somme, but you have to remember that he acted on advice from his staff and from a long chain of advisers. I don't think he was a butcher, it was just that we were men up against modern machine-guns. And although stated baldly it sounds mad to have walked across no man's land, arms aslant, remember that we thought the Germans had been knocked out and you can't run and dodge easily when you're carrying a rifle and masses of other gear.

As soon as we left our trenches we were hit badly and in some areas, of course, almost everyone was hit as soon as they began to move forward. My recollection as a stretcher-bearer was of men being hit all the time. It wasn't a question of a casualty now and then. As soon as we were over the top men were being bowled over left, right and centre. We would just go to the nearest one and see if he was able to walk back to our trenches. If not, we'd put him on the stretcher and carry him back, and of course all the time bullets would be flying all around us. Each stretcher-bearer only carried a field dressing, so with a badly injured man there was very little we could do other than get him away from the fighting as quickly as possible.

We were withdrawn from the fighting for about a week after we captured Montauban and when we returned to the front line it was to a spot in front of Bernafay Wood, a hundred or so yards beyond which was Trones Wood. I remember that before moving off from where we had spent the night, we had half-an-hour of physical jerks! Then, after our morning meal, we formed up in the open, and marched towards Bernafay Wood. We halted about 50 yards in front of the wood itself and then our commanding officer, as though on a parade ground, arranged for the companies to line out side by side and with a movement of his hand he signalled us to go forward. We had scarcely entered Bernafay Wood when all hell broke loose. There were machine-gun bullets flying everywhere and the enemy artillery simply pinned us so savagely that there was absolutely no possibility of moving forward at all. Eventually, our own artillery, which had been silent for some time, opened up and right behind it, as it lifted and moved forward, came the 2nd Wilts. They cleared the wood and it seemed to us that we'd simply been used to draw the enemy fire before the main assault. Again, while practically everything from that day in the way of detail has vanished, one incident does still come to the surface of my mind: my fellow stretcher-bearer and I were lying on the fringe of the wood when quite a big shell fell within a few inches of our feet. By a miracle it did not explode – had it done so, we would have been blown to pieces.

A fortnight later, my battalion was in action again, this time at Guillemont and only then was the division withdrawn from the Somme and moved to La Bassée sector, the 2nd Yorks occupying trenches at Givenchy. This area, like many other parts of the line, was a decidedly unhealthy place to be. No man's land at our sector was so narrow that in addition to the usual artillery shells we were able to lob trench and rifle mortars at each other across the narrow divide. But worst of all were the mines. Both sides would mine under each other's trenches and if you happened to be standing in that part of a trench immediately above a mine when it went off you had no chance. At least you could hear a shell coming, but with the mines you'd had it if you were in the wrong place at the wrong time. It was all right so long as both sides could hear each other digging. It was when the digging stopped that you had to start worrying because from then on you could expect to be blown sky high at any moment of the day or night.

By early October we were back on the Somme where, sometime in mid-October, I became a casualty. We were about to attack at a place near Warlencourt, but on the night before the battle was due to begin I took a casual walk between our forward and reserve trenches without using the proper communication trench.

Up on top I was, of course, vulnerable even though it was night-time and next thing I knew I'd been hit in the forearm. It may seem odd that I don't remember precisely where it happened but throughout the Great War ordinary soldiers very rarely knew where they were or where they were going. They were never told since their role was simply to fight and obey orders. Officers wouldn't have dreamed of telling their men where they were or why. You were just sent somewhere and you went. You didn't ask questions. The ordinary soldier who just moves where he is sent cannot often be sure where he is. Nor have I a clear recall of events leading to my arrival at a tented hospital which I believe was situated on the racecourse at Rouen, but I do remember, on coming to after a spell in the operation tent, seeing the medical officer at my bedside. He simply said, 'I've given you a blighty.' A few days later I was conveyed to a hospital ship on the river and bound, ultimately, for Southampton. I never went back to the front line after that because gangrene set in and I lost the use of my hand for some time. In fact I was lucky I didn't lose my hand.

During the crossing we, that is the wounded on board, were asked to what part of the UK we would like to be sent. That resulted in my being sent to a hospital in Warrington from where, after a short time, a week or so, I was transferred to another hospital in St Helens staffed in the main by nuns. By Christmas my wound was sufficiently healed for me to be discharged from hospital and, after the customary few days leave, I reported back to my regiment early in January 1917 at the Depot, Richmond. The Green Howard's Depot at Richmond was situated on a hill overlooking the town and one could see for miles; in fact, on a clear day, it was said that you could even see the tower of York Minster. I mention this merely to emphasize that it could be quite a bleak spot, particularly in January. So much so that on my first early morning parade, before breakfast, I fainted, whether from pain or the cold I don't know, but I was henceforth excused parades. Eventually I was sent to West Hartlepool from whence drafts, including casualties considered sufficiently recovered, were sent overseas, in other words back to the front. I, however, appeared before a Medical Board and was recommended for discharge with a 60 per cent disability pension. But because of the enormous casualties sustained in 1916, on the Somme in particular, instructions had been issued that those wounded who in the past might well have been discharged, should be used if at all possible in some non-combatant capacity. Their duties might include working in departmental corps, replacing fit men in those units who were about to go on active service. I was transferred to the Army Pay Corps and posted to Nottingham where a pay office had recently been opened to deal with the accounts of the Labour Corps. This would have been about April 1917 and I was employed there until the Armistice.

When peace came I was posted overseas to a pay office at Wimereux, near Boulogne. I had not been long here when men who had been out since 1914 were instructed to report to the orderly room of the unit. I duly reported and found that I had been discharged from the Army, with effect from July 1919. I was apparently surplus to military requirements. My pension was reduced to 10 per cent.

While in Nottingham I had undergone treatment to my injured arm at the city's general hospital. This had considerably improved my condition and I'd regained the use of my left hand – hence the reduction in the pension originally proposed. My pension ceased to be paid to me sometime in 1922 or 1923, following a policy referred to as the Geddes Axe. This was introduced by a cabinet minister of that name. Because of the financial state of the country all government and civil service employees had to take a 10 per cent cut in their salaries. As my arm had improved dramatically the Geddes Axe came down on my pension. I accepted the decision without protest.

After the war I worried about my lack of formal education so I taught myself French grammar and advertised in a Paris newspaper for a job teaching English to the French. I was offered a job but had in the meantime been offered a job with the Cunard shipping line in Paris. On 10 November 1939 I was specially re-enlisted by the Military Attaché in Paris and served throughout the Second World War in the Royal Engineers. I remained with Cunard in Paris till 1960 when I retired and returned first to Devon and then, finally, to Nottingham, to be near my son. Nottingham was my wife's home town.

INDEX